A
VOICE
FROM
JAPAN

BOOKS BY CAROLYN MEYER

Nonfiction

VOICES OF NORTHERN IRELAND:
Growing Up in a Troubled Land

VOICES OF SOUTH AFRICA:
Growing Up in a Troubled Land

THE MYSTERY OF THE ANCIENT MAYA
WITH CHARLES GALLENKAMP

AMISH PEOPLE:
Plain Living in a Complex World

THE CENTER:
From a Troubled Past to a New Life

THE BREAD BOOK:
All About Bread and How to Make It

MASK MAGIC

Fiction

DENNY'S TAPES

ELLIOTT & WIN

C. C. POINDEXTER

EULALIA'S ISLAND

THE SUMMER I LEARNED ABOUT LIFE

THE LUCK OF TEXAS McCOY

A VOICE FROM JAPAN

An Outsider Looks In

Carolyn Meyer

Gulliver Books

Harcourt Brace Jovanovich

San Diego   New York   London

HBJ

Library of Congress Cataloging-in-Publication Data
Meyer, Carolyn.
  A voice from Japan: an outsider looks in/by Carolyn Meyer.
    p. cm.
  "Gulliver books."
  Bibliography: p.
  Includes index.
  Summary: The author relates her visit to Japan where she
interviewed adults and children and recorded their feelings about
life in a country experiencing drastic changes in lifestyle.
  ISBN 0-15-200633-8
  1. Japan—Description and travel—1945–   2. Japan—Social life and
customs—1945–   3. Children—Japan. 4. Meyer, Carolyn—Journeys—
Japan. [1. Japan—Social life and customs. 2. Japan—Description
and travel.] I. Title.
DS811.M49 1988
952.04—dc19   88-2286

Printed in the United States of America

First edition

A B C D E

To Ernest G. and Rebecca D. Mares

Contents

CONTENTS

CONTENTS

CONTENTS

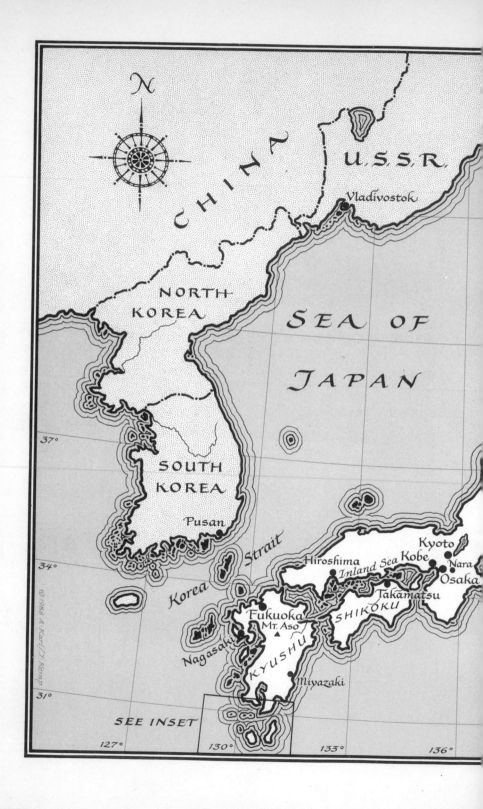

Prologue: On the Inside

Gina

"**I** really want to write a book about this!"
Gina is an eighteen-year-old Canadian exchange student halfway through her one-year stay in Japan. She has been there long enough to understand what is going on but not long enough to stop noticing differences. And she has kept a journal since her arrival in Japan.

"I lived with my family for four months before they stopped treating me like a guest and let me do anything," she said, "and it's only for the last month or so that I've seen the family as it really is, and not just as they want me to see them."

Gina, long-legged, blue-eyed, blond, and outgoing, stands out in Japan. What's most outstanding, though, is her flexibility. She is remarkably adept not only at speaking

Japanese but at picking up on unspoken rules. She has learned to read faces to figure out what is really meant.

"I found out the hard way that *yes* in Japan often means *no*. The Japanese rarely say no. They expect others to understand when they mean no, even when they say yes.

"When I first arrived, I knew I was expected to ask Okā-san, my host mother, for permission whenever I wanted to go somewhere. Okā-san always said yes, and I took her at her word and went to meet a friend, or see a movie, or whatever it was. After a couple of weeks of this, the school advisor called me and explained that my host mother didn't mean yes at all and was very angry with me, but wouldn't say anything. She expected me to *know* that she disapproved." Confrontation is avoided in Japan, but Gina forced it anyway: "I insisted that Okā-san sit down with me once a week to talk about problems."

"Does it work?" I asked.

"No," she admitted. "She still won't say what she means. She and my advisor are always discussing me behind my back—they never say anything to my face. But I've gotten better at understanding the messages."

It's not easy when you're eighteen to submit to rules laid down for sixteen-year-old Japanese girls, who are treated more like American twelve-year-olds. "The family is very protective of me. I'm not allowed to go out with boys, of course. That didn't surprise me. But I'm also not allowed to eat raw carrots, because Okā-san insists they're not good for me. I go along with the rule about boys, but I buy my own vegetables."

Dozo, an expression that means "please," is used to invite people to come in, to have a seat, to have a second helping of food. "When people say '*dozo*,' they don't really mean it," Gina said. "Sometimes when Okā-san is really busy, on her way out to work or something, and someone stops by, she says, 'Dozo, *dozo,*' and I know she doesn't want them to come in and visit, but she won't ever just say, 'I'm sorry, I'm on my way to work—can you come back another time?' The Japanese have two faces: one for the family, one for the outside world. I'd be appalled if my own mother behaved that way, but here that's what's expected.

"I learned that when I speak English, it hurts Okā-san's feelings. I stopped calling my real mother in Canada, because Okā-san interprets both the phone call and the English conversation as criticism. I used to go out with other families, then come back and talk about the great time I had. But I learned that my enthusiasm made Okā-san feel she wasn't trying hard enough, that the family wasn't doing enough. So now when I come back I just say, 'It was nice, but I'm glad to be home.' "

Gina was fascinated with the idea that I was writing a book about Japan, and she wanted to talk. I was delighted to have an opportunity to listen to a real insider who had a teenager's perspective. Gina invited me to visit on an afternoon when her host mother was at work and would not be offended when we spoke English and laughed together. It was a welcome relief for me. I didn't have to be conscious of how I sat or waved my hands, or to wonder if I was laughing too loudly. I had been in Japan only a couple of weeks when I met Gina, and I was already exhausted from worrying constantly about whether I was behaving properly. I admired Gina: not only had she learned to speak fluent Japanese in a short time, but she had adjusted to many of their expectations. I was not sure I could have done so well.

"So what's it like here, Gina?"

Deep breath.

"The parents are workaholics. They're hardly ever home. They own a shop that sells all kinds of decorations. As you can see from this house, it's a good business. They have five children, three of them gone and two—sixteen-year-old twins, a boy and a girl—still at home. The three older kids all went through universities. Someone comes in to do the cleaning. They don't want me to, but I insist on helping with the cooking. That shamed the son and daughter into doing something, too.

"When I first got here, I was astonished to see how the Japanese girls cling together in bunches, holding hands and giggling. The boys hang around together, too. I've gotten to know some of the girls, and I'm beginning to learn more and more about the importance of the group. And I'm changing, too. When I go home I'll be much different, not so much the all-for-myself individual I used to be. My real mother in Canada doesn't quite understand what's happening to me.

"One of the first things the Japanese girls asked me was about my boyfriends at home. I have a special friend, Matt; we've known each other for years, and they always refer to him as my 'lover.' Their assumption is that all American girls have at least a half-dozen boyfriends and sleep with them all. The Japanese have a lot of stereotypes about North Americans, and the other way around. I don't want to be a teacher, but I do want to come back here after college and find some way to work as an intercultural bridge between Japan and the West. There was a story recently about the wife of an executive who committed suicide because she found out she was going to have to go to the United States with her husband; she couldn't bear the thought of the culture shock—it was too much for her. I want to find a way to work with people to prevent this.

"Kids here talk about sex constantly. The boys are really letches! They talk about girls in sexual ways all the time. Nobody has friends of the opposite sex—boys think of sex and girls think of romance. The boys aren't the only ones who think American girls are sexually very free. So do the teachers! I'm very resentful of the attitude of some of the male teachers in my school. At first I thought maybe I was just reading the situation wrong, but then I checked with some of the other exchange students and found out they had had the same experiences. The teachers don't actually come on, but they make it clear that they'd like to.

"I'm tempted to say that Japanese teenagers are immature, but that sounds like some kind of value judgment. Let's just say that in comparison to North Americans, Japanese teen-agers haven't learned to take responsibility, to take care of themselves, to make their own decisions, to help around the house. And they like it that way. I heard a girl say, 'I don't want to be twenty; then I won't be a child anymore.' Smart kids don't want to grow up. And I don't blame them, because from then on the responsibilities are really heavy.

"The worst thing, though, is the way the kids treat their parents. They talk back to them, they abuse them, they order them around. Kids expect their parents to wait on them, and they do absolutely nothing to help around the house. They're spoiled rotten. And not just the kids in my family; all the kids I've met are that way. They get big allowances, and all they have to do is ask for more.

"Japanese kids lie to their parents a lot, saying that they're going to the library to study when actually they're sneaking out to meet someone. I'd rather have a more open relation-ship with parents, telling them where I'm actually going and why and when I'll be back—and being allowed to do it. That's the way it is at home.

"You should hear how the kids in this family speak to their parents. They call the mother 'shithead.' This is a fifty-three-year-old woman who works in her own business, seven days a week. Even if she didn't, she'd be entitled to some kind of respect. I've seen the sixteen-year-old daughter yank the newspaper out of her mother's hands when her mother is reading it. The kids definitely run the family, and this is true in other families I've met too. Everything is totally focused on those kids, feeding them, clothing them, indulging them, but not allowing them any kind of freedom.

"My 'sister' who is so surly and snotty around the house is a totally different person at school and around her friends. She's very warm and considerate to them. It's hard to believe. Back to the idea that everybody here has two ways of operating, one for the family and a totally different way for the outside world.

"I'm not sure how much Japanese students actually study. Like lots of Americans, they sometimes do a lot of crash studying right before an exam, but there are others who are very serious and want to go to top universities, and they study constantly. My 'brother' never studies. He plays video games all the time. If he studies an hour a month, that's the max. But he'll still have to go to some kind of college, or maybe a technical school. There's no social prestige in just making it through high school. He'll be sent somewhere to get a degree of some kind.

"I know this all sounds harsh, but that's because it's so *different*. This family would do anything for me. A few weeks ago I got sick and had to go to the hospital. I was scared to death! I hurt so much, I couldn't explain to the doctors what was wrong, and I didn't understand what the doctors were saying. I had appendicitis, and Okā-san stayed in the hospital with me the whole time. She made them put a cot in my room so she could sleep there. And since I've gotten out, she treats me like a baby. I missed my own mother, but I don't know how I could have survived without Okā-san.

"It's really an amazing place, Japan. Somebody said to

me once, 'When you've been in Japan for seven days, it all seems very strange, and you realize you don't understand how the society works at all. Then when you've been in Japan for seven months, you think you've got it all figured out. And when you've been in Japan for seven years, you realize that you don't understand it at all.' "

"Do you get lonely?" I asked, thinking about what a strain it must be on her to live like this.

"Sure. All the exchange students do. I'm as 'inside' as I'm ever going to get in Japan, right here in the heart of a family that really cares about me. But there's nothing lonelier than living in the midst of a group of people who don't have the faintest idea of what you're really like."

In the spring of 1987, I sat in the New York office of a foundation known for its connections with Japan. I hoped to leave four months later for Japan, and so far I had no idea how I was going to approach the problem of doing research for a book in a country where I could speak not one word of the language and knew not one person.

At that point I was confident—well, *fairly* confident—that I could do it. This would not be the first time I had taken on a difficult writing assignment. In the fall of 1985, gripped by inflamed headlines about racial turmoil in South Africa, I had traveled to that country to find out how such turmoil affected young people growing up there. Weeks later I had returned home, emotionally involved in South Africa's problems and deeply troubled by what I had seen. As a result of that experience, I wrote *Voices of South Africa: Growing Up in a Troubled Land*. Late in the spring of 1986, caught up in newspaper stories of the seemingly endless Troubles in Northern Ireland, I visited the country, again concerned about the effects of the violence on young people. I came home from that trip saddened by the apparent hopelessness of the situation and wrote a second book, *Voices of Northern Ireland*. The subtitle remained the same: *Growing Up in a Troubled Land*.

Then, intrigued by magazine stories and television specials about Japan—about the incredible economic growth that had propelled the country to the top of the world, about the educational system that many people think is closely connected with that growth—I decided to spend a month there. South Africa had angered me, Northern Ireland had depressed me, Japan fascinated and intellectually challenged me.

When I went to South Africa and then to Northern Ireland, I had started with the names of a couple of people. They had led me to others, and soon I had a network of people to help me. I thought I could use the same approach in Japan. The foundation executive disagreed.

"It won't work," he said. "If you don't have the proper contacts in Japan, your charming smile will get you nowhere. It doesn't matter who you are. And if you just flit from place to place, no one will take you seriously. They'll treat you like a tourist and you won't learn a thing."

His assistant stuck her head in the door. "I'll give her Jackson Bailey's address."

Jackson Bailey, it turned out, is Professor of History at Earlham College in Richmond, Indiana, and director of the school's Institute for Education on Japan. For the past century, Earlham has been sending graduates to teach in Japan, and young Japanese have been studying on the Richmond campus. I wrote to Dr. Bailey, explained what I was doing, sent him a résumé to show what I had done in the past (this résumé was to haunt me later), and asked for his help.

Not much happened for a month or two. Just as I was beginning to panic, Bailey sent me copies of letters he had written to people in Japan—one to the director of International House in Tokyo for a place to stay when I was in that city, another to an American teacher in Tokyo, a third to a Japanese colleague in the small city of Utsunomiya (pronounced OOHT-s'noh-mee-yah). About a hundred kilometers (sixty-two miles) north of Tokyo, the city is not remote, but it is far enough away to have a character of its own; that's where Bailey thought I should establish my base.

I wrote follow-up letters to Bailey's contacts, as well as to other people I regarded as long shots—friends of friends, mostly Americans. I described my other two *Voices* books and explained that I wanted to write about young Japanese and what it's like to grow up in Japanese society.

July passed with no response from anyone. I had already bought my plane ticket and gotten my visa. I sent off another round of letters, trying to sound urgent but not hysterical. When I tried calling Jackson Bailey, I learned he was in a cabin in Vermont without a telephone. I settled down to practice what I hoped was Oriental patience.

Then came a letter from Mr. Kawahara, an administrator with the board of education in Utsunomiya. In longhand on several sheets of soft Japanese paper, he outlined the plans that were being made for me for two intense weeks of visits to schools and families. He had been recruited by Dr. Bailey's colleague, Mrs. Murata.

Mitsuo (MEE-tsoh), a student whom I had met through an international program at the University of New Mexico, brought me a list of the people in his older sister's family. "Please visit them when you are in Tokyo," he said. "It is a typical Japanese family."

Next, Louise, the American teacher, wrote that she had some ideas for my stay in Tokyo. Friends of friends who were teaching in Japan said to call them when I got there and they would try to help me out in Kyoto. Mrs. Takagi, a writer visiting Albuquerque, asked me to come to see her in Fukuoka. Masako (MAH-sah-koh), another student whom I had met at the University of New Mexico, invited me to stay with her in Miyazaki. All of these places were merely dots on a map to me.

Days before I was to leave, Professor Amemiya, a teacher of English at a university in Tokyo with whom I had corresponded years ago, answered my letter. He wrote that he would be out of the country when I arrived, but that if I would wire flight information, he would send two students to meet my plane—a young college student named Maiko (MY-koh) and an older graduate student, Mr. Shirota.

Somehow it had all come together. On Saturday, August 30, I left home, crossed the international date line, and on Sunday, August 31, I was in Japan. Maiko carried a sign that said CAROLYN MEYER!! COME HERE!! Groggy after thirteen hours on the plane, I nearly missed her sign. She presented a bouquet of roses, and Mr. Shirota led me to his car. Both spoke English. They wanted to help.

During the weeks that followed, with the help of Maiko and Mr. Shirota and dozens of others, I accumulated a vast amount of information of all kinds. I learned about Japanese language and culture and how they reflect Japan's history; about Japanese education, both good and bad; about families and the significance of "insiders" and "outsiders."

There were problems, however. The barriers of language and culture proved formidable. The "voices" were often distorted by translation or obscured by the formality of the situation. Young people in Japan are simply not accustomed to open, informal conversation with adults, even in their own language.

Race and religion had simplified writing about South Africa and Northern Ireland, but the absence of clear issues made organizing what I learned about Japan like putting together a gigantic jigsaw puzzle with thousands of tiny pieces, like assembling a complex mosaic. Although I made good friends among the Japanese, I knew that I would never be "inside," in the way that Gina is. Still, as an outsider, I was fortunate to be offered unusual and often intimate glimpses of a society so fundamentally different from ours. The "voice" from Japan is my own.

Part One

JAPAN AND THE REST OF THE WORLD

1
Becoming Number One

Yoko

About fifteen girls were gathered in the Utsunomiya Girls' High School conference room one afternoon after class. A thunderstorm crashed and boomed outside the window, sometimes drowning out conversation. Nearly half the students had had the experience of studying abroad for a year. Yoko, a forthright girl in glasses and a Michigan State sweatshirt, became the speaker for the group, although on most subjects they were not reluctant to give their own opinions. They complained that their host families in America had expected too much of them—Japanese teenagers generally don't help much around the house. Some complained about rich, greasy American food that had made them sick until they'd gotten used to it (and learned to enjoy it).

But some things they really liked: they talked about how

3

much freedom there is in American schools, how friendly American students are. "American boys used to hug me and ask, 'How are you doing, Yoko?' That's something a Japanese boy would *never* do."

It was a good session until I committed an error. I had been told that most graduates of this high school went on to a university, and that the emphasis was on getting into a good university rather than choosing a career. So I asked, "Which universities would you like to go to?"

Silence fell, broken only by a couple of nervous giggles. "That's not a question you ask here," Yoko said. "No one ever talks about that."

So I apologized and backed off. The reason, I learned later, was that Japanese don't like to risk embarrassment or rejection. To admit a preference for one of the leading universities—Todai or Waseda, for example—and then to be turned down would be humiliating. I was curious to see how high these bright girls were aiming in a country where women are traditionally discriminated against, but their reaction to my question made me feel I had blundered into something terribly personal, like asking how much money their fathers earned.

The city of Utsunomiya does not find its way into tourist guidebooks, except as a place to change trains for somewhere more interesting. Surrounded by rice fields, it lies on a broad plain, the sea forty miles to the east, spectacular mountains an hour's drive to the northwest. With a population approaching half a million, this high-tech manufacturing city is also the capital of Tochigi Prefecture (Japan is divided into forty-seven prefectures, called *ken*, similar to our states). The meandering Tagawa River cuts through the center of town.

Mrs. Murata, my chief contact in Utsunomiya, met my

train, the high-speed Shinkansen ("bullet train") from Toyko, drove me to a small hotel on the main street a few blocks from the station, and presented my agenda. It was detailed to the minute: where I was to be and when, what time she would pick me up, whom I would meet when I got there—morning, noon, and night for fourteen days. Mrs. Murata would act as interpreter when she was needed. She became my friend and confidante as well, but although for two weeks we were together every day, we never called each other by our first names.

The scenario became familiar. I would arrive at a school with Mrs. Murata, take off my shoes and leave them at the entrance (sometimes in a cubbyhole, sometimes simply lined up by the step), and then put on the slippers provided. Mrs. Murata would introduce me to the welcome committee, and we would all bow. Then someone, the head teacher or the English teacher, would conduct me—SLIPslop, SLIPslop—to the principal's office.

Those offices all looked the same: a large room with a big desk and chair, two sofas facing each other across a coffee table. Sometimes there were old-fashioned crocheted doilies on the arms of the sofas and on the table. I would be introduced to the principal, always male, usually in his late fifties, and I would bow and say "Hajime mashite" (HAH-jee-meh MAHSH-teh), meaning "How do you do?" Other people—assistant principals, head teachers, English teachers—would be introduced, we would all bow again, and I would be shown to the seat of honor at the coffee table. A secretary or a nervous student would appear with cups of green tea. The cups have no handles, and only the principal and I got saucers, subtle status symbols.

We would exchange meishi (MAY-shee), business cards with name and address that are indispensable in Japan. They must be presented correctly, so that the person receiving

5

the *meishi* can read your name and, more importantly, your title; this is how the Japanese figure out your rank and importance, and how they know exactly what degree of formal courtesy to extend to you—how low to bow, how politely to speak. Of course I couldn't read theirs or even tell top from bottom.

One of the English teachers would act as interpreter, probably dreading the situation. We would make polite, stilted conversation for a long time, often referring to copies of my résumé that everyone seemed to have. At Mrs. Murata's suggestion, I always took a copy of *Voices of South Africa* to pass around. "It's an impressive *meishi*," she said. "It shows them you can do what you say you do."

It did no good to get restless during the seemingly endless formalities, because this was how the Japanese operated. Maybe there would be a tour of the school, and eventually a chance to meet some students, which was what I had come for.

The meetings with students were basically the same, too—very formal. We always met in a conference room, the tables usually arranged around an open square. There was often a bunch of fresh flowers in the room, sometimes on a table in the middle of the square, sometimes next to the Honored Guest (me). The prize pupils who had been drafted to come to meet the American visitor would look at me expectantly, most of them hoping fervently they wouldn't have to speak English.

Fortunately, not all the students were so reticent. Utsunomiya Girls' High School (or UJK, from its Japanese initials) was different in a number of ways. Most public schools are coeducational, but UJK has been a girls' school since its founding in 1875. Most high schools require students to wear uniforms, but the UJK girls were as casually dressed as American students. Still, there are rules: no permed hair, no jewelry, no makeup, no tight skirts or sleeveless dresses. The school has an excellent academic reputation, and girls from all over the prefecture compete for admission. There are about twelve hundred students in three grades.

I don't like meeting with large groups—I prefer to meet with two or three people in an informal setting. But that was often hard to arrange, and as large groups go, the one at UJK was working out rather well, even with my question about their university ambitions. By four-thirty the rain had stopped. I thought maybe they'd want to leave, but when I mentioned that they were free to go, they all said they wanted to keep talking. So I encouraged *them* to ask the questions.

Once again it was Yoko who jumped right in. "How does it feel to know that Japan is Number One and America isn't anymore?"

Yoko might not make it as a diplomat, but she was aware (as are most young Japanese) of her country's phenomenal progress, from a state of near-total devastation at the end of World War II in 1945 to being one of the most productive nations in the world. *Fortune's* 1987 list of the 500 largest corporations outside the United States includes 152 in Japan. Japan's unemployment rate is 3 percent, compared to about 6 percent in the U.S. Its rate of economic growth is stronger than ours.

But I was still not prepared to agree that Japan was now Number One. Yoko, however, was not alone in her opinion: it's what most Japanese believe. I had an answer ready for this question, which came up often in one form or another. History works in cycles, I told Yoko and her classmates— countries and cultures go through phases. The United States has ridden the crest of world power for a long time; Japan has been on an upswing and is nearing that crest. But even as it thinks of itself as Number One, a new cycle is beginning. The obsessive dedication to work that propelled Japan to the top is starting to wane. Yielding to pressure from workers, the government plans to shorten the standard work week of forty-eight hours to forty within the next few years. Many young people no longer want to devote their lives to their jobs—they want more leisure time.

To understand Japan's rise as a world power, it's necessary to take a look at its geography and history. Japan is a relatively small country in terms of size, a string of islands lying directly west of the United States on the opposite side of the Pacific Ocean. Japanese students are surprised and offended that American students don't seem to know where Japan is and can't even find it on a world map. The archipelago runs roughly northeast to southwest off the Asian continent, separated from the Soviet Union and Korea by the Sea of Japan, several hundred miles wide. A map of Japan laid over a map of the east coast of North America stretches roughly from Montreal to Montgomery, Alabama.

There are four main islands. Honshu is the largest, crescent-shaped with all of the great cities in Japan strung out along its curving, Pacific-facing side: Tokyo, Yokohama, Kyoto, Osaka, Hiroshima. Hokkaido, primarily a rural area, lies to the north. The best-known city there is Sapporo, where the Winter Olympics were held in 1972. A line drawn from Sapporo to Tokyo runs north-south, but from Tokyo to Hiroshima, east-west. Kyushu, the farthest south and west of the four islands, is smaller than Hokkaido, lying so close to the western end of Honshu that you barely notice when the train crosses from one to the other. Shikoku, the smallest island, is separated from Honshu by the Inland Sea. The oceans around Japan are peppered with many tiny islands including Okinawa, but even on the largest island, no place is more than seventy miles from the sea. The climate ranges from the fierce winters of the north to the semitropical weather of the south. Snow falls heavily in the mountainous regions. Summers are generally hot and humid; winters, cold and damp.

The total land area is 142,811 square miles, smaller than the state of Montana (147,000 square miles). Steep mountains, many of them volcanic, cover about two-thirds of the land surface of Japan, and only about a fifth of it is flat enough to cultivate. In the narrow valleys between the mountains and along the coastal plains live 122 million people, about half the population of the United States. The density of population is the highest in the world.

Rice is the main crop, raised throughout Japan, and the area around Utsunomiya is a particularly good rice-growing region. By early September the harvest had begun, the rice stalks cut and hung on wooden racks to dry, leaving behind rows of stubble that looked like a worn-out hairbrush. In other areas the rice was still in the fields, turning a pale yellow, with a colorful variety of scarecrows to keep the birds from eating the grain.

The growing season is long, but the soil is not particularly rich, and farmers use fertilizers abundantly. Nevertheless, growers expected a bumper crop of rice for the fourth straight year in 1987, and the government had to decide what to do with the oversupply. The Japanese pay more for their rice than people in any other country in the world because of government price-support systems that help the rice farmers but keep the cost to consumers high. California farmers grow the same type of rice as that raised in Japan and offer it for sale at a fraction of the price, but the Japanese government will not allow the importation of American rice to compete with their own product. The artificially high cost of rice is a hotly debated topic in Japan.

Some farmers grow vegetables and keep a few beef cattle,

but like many island nations, Japan must import much of its food and almost all of its raw materials for manufacturing. Soybeans, which provide the basic protein of the Japanese diet in the form of *tofu*, a soft white curd, and *miso*, fermented bean paste used to make broth, are also imported, primarily from the United States. Japan has hardly any mineral resources, and the country is totally dependent on imported petroleum.

Japan is now even importing chopsticks. Except when dining out in a foreign restaurant, Japanese eat with chopsticks, usually disposable wooden ones, going through about 130 million pairs every day. But even with all the forest-covered mountains, Japan's supply of clean, white wood suitable for chopsticks is dwindling. A plant in Minnesota now churns out 7 million pairs of chopsticks a day to ship to Japan.

The prehistory of Japan is shrouded in myth and explained in legend. *Japan*, incidentally, is the English name for the country, from Chinese words meaning "land of the rising sun." The official Japanese name for the country is *Nihon; ni* means "sun," and so this is again "land of the rising sun." Another Japanese name for the country is *Nippon*, short for *Nippon-koku*, "land of the origin of the sun." The story goes that Japan was originally founded in 660 B.C. by Emperor Jimmu, said to be a direct descendant of the sun goddess and the divine ancestor of all the later emperors, including the present one, Hirohito. This story was official dogma until the end of World War II, when Emperor Hirohito announced to his subjects that he was not divine, a declaration they greeted with equanimity.

A more accurate explanation of Japan's prehistory is that modern Japanese are a Mongoloid people, like other Asiatics. Physical characteristics include yellowish skin, medium stature, straight dark hair, sparse body hair, and a fold of skin in the eyelid called the epicanthic fold, which gives the Asiatic eye an almond shape. The ancestors of present-day Japanese arrived in the islands as part of a migration from northeastern Asia that moved down through the Korean Peninsula and across the Korea Strait into Kyushu and western Honshu. There was also an influx of arrivals from southeast Asia. These newcomers overcame the aboriginal *Ainu* (EYE-nooh), who were physically similar to Caucasians and much hairier than Mongoloids, and eventually conquered them, driving the few remaining Ainu into the northern reaches of Hokkaido, where their descendants still live.

As you might suppose, living in a country broken up by towering mountains into small plains and valleys and surrounded by water, the early inhabitants formed numerous clans or tribal kingdoms, each with its own chieftain (some female) who had religious functions. Around the first century A.D., people crossing the Korea Strait brought with them bronze and iron implements. Some historians think this may have happened a couple of hundred years earlier. In any case, metal tools did not arrive in Japan until hundreds or maybe a thousand or more years after the Europeans and Middle Easterners had learned to use metal. The Koreans also brought with them a system of agriculture.

Between the fifth and sixth centuries A.D., a clan that may have come originally from Kyushu settled on the Nara Plain (sometimes called the Yamato Plain) in the middle of Honshu, near what is now the city of Kyoto. This Yamato clan took charge, claiming leadership of all the clans in central and western Japan. Over the next couple of centuries, civilization developed in that area, borrowing a great deal from China, including the Buddhist religion. In the seventh century the world's oldest wooden structure, Hoyuji Temple, was built in the style of China's elegant T'ang dynasty. The upper classes of Japan, much in love with everything Chinese, devoted themselves to the study of Chinese language and culture. Until then, the Japanese had been lagging far behind the Europeans in literature, philosophy, art, science, and government, but now the Japanese passed the Europeans in a blaze of Chinese-inspired glory.

The head of the Yamato clan began to think of himself as a divine emperor and had a beautiful Chinese-style capital city erected at Nara, quite an accomplishment for a society that until then had not even bothered to build towns. At the end of the eighth century the capital was moved to a new city laid out in a neat Chinese checkerboard pattern with a palace in the center. The city was named Heian, and the next few centuries were called the Heian period. The capital was later renamed Kyoto. Remnants of that splendid period make present-day Kyoto one of the handsomest cities in contemporary Japan.

Meanwhile, in those early centuries, feudalism was on the rise. Feudalism, the political and economic system that dominated Europe from the ninth to fifteenth centuries, also developed in other civilizations when conditions were similar: some men became landholders and needed others to work the land; both the noblemen who owned the land and the peasants who farmed it needed armed protection. The principle in Japan was much the same. The *daimyo* (DY-myoh), meaning "great name," were feudal barons, landholders who had been building up huge estates since the eighth century. Clans fought among themselves until one of the daimyo defeated his rivals and set up a military dictatorship, calling himself *shōgun* (SHOH-gun), which translates as "barbarian-subduing generalissimo." A military government took over at the end of the twelfth century, ruling in the name of the shōgun. And the shōgun, at least in theory, got his power from the emperor in Kyoto.

In feudal Japan, society was rigidly divided into five classes. At the top were the daimyo, the lords. Under them were *samurai* (SAH-mooh-ry), well-trained warriors who were their knights. Next came the peasants, the artisans, and, at the bottom, the merchants. Not included in this rigid caste system were the outcasts, the *eta*, who did the dirty jobs that no one else would do—gathering night soil, working in slaughterhouses, tanning leather.

The samurai were the aristocrats of the twelfth century; it was their privilege to wear two swords, and they had life-and-death control over commoners, beheading on the spot anyone on lower rungs of the social ladder who might offend them. They trained rigorously to withstand pain and physical hardship, and they were as willing to die themselves as they were to cause the death of others. They swore loyalty to their daimyo, but it was the samurai who ran the show. Sometimes, after the death of their daimyo, the samurai found themselves without an overlord. These masterless samurai were called *ronin*, and often they became roving bands of bandits. Today in Japan, *ronin* is the term for young men (and most are males) who have failed their university entrance exams and are taking a year or two to study before they try again. When they eventually pass their exams, they will be loyal to the university that accepts them; later they will transfer that same loyalty to the company that hires them. Thus, parallels to feudalism can sometimes be found in present-day Japanese society.

Twice in the thirteenth century, Japan was threatened with invasion—the only times in its history until World War II. The Mongols, under the leadership of Kublai Khan, had marauded through most of Asia and the Middle East; Japan was next on their list. But as the Mongolian fleet sailed across the Korea Strait, a typhoon—the Japanese equivalent of a hurricane—whirled up out of the South Pacific and

13

smashed the invaders' ships. The Japanese called that typhoon *kamikaze* (KAH-mee-kah-zeh) meaning "divine wind." Six centuries later they gave the name kamikaze to suicide pilots who were ordered to crash their planes loaded with bombs into American ships.

Between the fourteenth and sixteenth centuries there were historical ups and downs, battles among feuding factions, but eventually a shōgun of the Tokugawa family was able to unite Japan under a stable system. Edo, meaning "eastern capital," was the early name for Tokyo, where the Tokugawa shogunate moved its capital in 1603. This began the Edo period. For the next 250 years the shogunate wielded almost absolute political power. Some of the shōgun had become more powerful than the emperor himself, who claimed divine descent from the sun goddess. Japan was a country ruled by warriors.

But change was on the way. By the end of the Edo period, the merchants were rising from the very bottom of the feudal system, gaining in power as the economy developed. The daimyo had acquired a taste for luxury, and the lowly merchants were only too happy to indulge that taste. To pay for their luxuries, landlords leaned harder and harder on the peasants who worked their lands and who were forced to hand over more and more of their rice harvest to the daimyo. Meanwhile, the samurai had become parasites, fatcat bureaucrats who also lived off the peasants. The daimyo fell deeper into debt, and the scorned merchants became richer and more powerful. The feudal system began to fall apart.

All this time Japan had managed successfully to remain isolated. This isolation had profound effects on Japanese society. It kept the society genetically "pure" and unchanged; for centuries no new genes came into the country to alter the physical makeup of the Japanese people. And

14

since their love affair with Chinese culture in the eighth century, no new foreign ideas had been introduced.

As a result, Japan is one of the most homogeneous countries in the world. Compare it to the United States, long described as a "melting pot." Some of the ingredients in our "pot" have blended while others have remained distinct, but the result is a rich mixture. The Japanese view their homogeneity as a strength. Certainly this homogeneity has made it easier for them to change direction as a nation, as they have demonstrated at various times in their history; it also makes communication with one another easier, since everybody understands intuitively what is being said. But this same homogeneity creates an "insider-outsider" mentality: Everyone not born and raised Japanese is considered *gaijin* (GY-jeen), meaning "outsider," someone who can't possibly understand what Japan and the Japanese are all about.

Total isolation couldn't last. Portuguese sailors arriving in 1542 made the first European contact, followed in a few years by Jesuit missionaries who converted some three hundred thousand Japanese to Catholicism. This injection of Western ideas was threatening to some. The Tokugawa daimyo ruling in 1638 ordered the death of most of the converted Christians and prohibited all further contact with foreign countries, except for a Dutch trading post in Nagasaki. For the next two hundred years Japan remained completely cut off from the outside world. No Japanese were allowed to go abroad, and those who had gone before the new ruling were not allowed to return for fear of contamination. The isolation was almost complete—but not quite. The few who knew what they were missing kept in touch with scientific and intellectual developments in Europe through Dutch books smuggled in by the traders in Nagasaki.

Then came Commodore Perry.

Matthew C. Perry had a long and distinguished career in the U.S. Navy behind him when he was given the tricky assignment of forcing Japan to open the country to foreign trade. For years American ships had been sailing past Japan on their way to trade with China or hunt whales. Persuasion had been attempted and hadn't succeeded, and the American government decided to try a show of strength.

On July 8, 1853, Perry anchored his four naval vessels—two of them powerful steam warships—in Edo Bay (Tokyo was still called Edo at that time). The Japanese ordered him to sail on to Nagasaki. Perry refused. Instead, he presented a letter from President Millard Fillmore to the Japanese emperor. The letter asked the Japanese to protect shipwrecked American sailors, to sell coal (one of Japan's few natural resources) to the United States, and to open at least one port for trade with the West. It was more of an order than a request.

Then Perry and his ships moved to the coast of China and waited. He was joined by more ships—almost a quarter of the U.S. Navy was with him—and in February the huge American fleet sailed back to Edo. The Tokugawa emperor bowed to the inevitable. At the end of March 1854, a treaty was signed accepting all of the American demands, and two ports were opened for trade. But the treaty that was signed was unequal, heavily weighted in favor of the United States.

Until then the Tokugawa shogunate held the real power in Japan, and the emperor was a shadowy figure stashed away in Kyoto. New anti-Tokugawa forces rising to power looked to the past for ways of dealing with the foreign threat. In 1868 the shogunate finally collapsed, and the emperor, a fifteen-year-old boy, was "restored" to power. He was given the name Meiji (MAY-jee), and the brilliant period that followed is known as the Meiji Restoration. The imperial capital was transferred from Kyoto to Edo. Under imaginative new leadership, Japanese society made a sudden about-face and moved off in a radically new direction.

Operating on the "If you can't fight 'em, join 'em" theory, the new rulers made no attempt to expel the foreigners moving into their country. Instead they began to adopt many aspects of Western civilization, just as centuries earlier Japan had absorbed many aspects of Chinese culture. One of their first acts in 1871 was to abolish feudalism, eliminating all legal inequality among classes. Not everyone was pleased with the reforms, of course, but their exceptional leaders accomplished a great deal in a short time. They sent people to Europe and the United States to study military science; these emissaries came home and created a modern army and navy. Others went to learn about economics and finance; they returned and established a banking system and issued new currency. They learned about education and set up a compulsory public school system. They reformed the calendar. They studied the Prussian constitution and drew up one like it, establishing an elected legislative body called the Diet.

But while some scholars were coming back from their studies abroad with new ideas, others were digging into the past and resurrecting old myths. They proclaimed the emperor divine and demanded loyalty to him.

It's hardly surprising that as the Japanese took on so many positive aspects of Western civilization, they would inevitably pick up some of the negatives, too. And they did: they began to practice imperialism, "the extension of rule or influence by one government, nation, or society over another." Any country that colonizes another is practicing imperialism, and this was a time when many European governments were establishing colonies in Africa, South America, India, and islands of the Far East. By forcing Japan to end its isolationist policies, the United States committed an act of imperialism. And from the beginning, the Japanese showed they were fast learners.

In 1894, Japan fought with China over control of Korea in the first Sino-Japanese War. In 1904, Japan and Russia, two imperial powers, fought over Manchuria and Korea. To the surprise of the Russians and the rest of the world, Japan speedily crushed the Russian fleet and was recognized as a world power. Five years after that war ended, heady with triumph, Japan annexed Korea. Another five years later, in 1915, they went to work on China, trying to reduce that giant nation to a protectorate but never quite succeeding.

Over the next decade or so, Japan concentrated on internal affairs. During the 1930s, the power of the military party gradually increased, until by the fall of 1941 the militarists were in complete control. On December 7, 1941, without warning, Japan bombed Pearl Harbor, Hawaii, where most of the U.S. Pacific Fleet was anchored. The next day the United States declared war on Japan.

Over the months that followed, Japan gained control of most of the Pacific. Then, slowly, the tide began to turn. Islands once lost to the Japanese were retaken, and fire-bombings of Japanese cities began. On August 6, 1945, the United States dropped an atomic bomb on the industrial city of Hiroshima; three days later another bomb was dropped on Nagasaki. On August 14, the emperor spoke to his people over the radio and renounced his claim to divinity. Japan surrendered.

The American occupation forces arrived in Japan under the leadership of General Douglas MacArthur. Sometimes called "American samurai," the occupation forces brought about radical changes in every area of Japanese life. First on the list, of course, was demilitarization. But changes in the educational system were instituted: schools were made coeducational, compulsory education was extended to nine years, and the American system of three years each of junior high and high school was imposed. The principle of equality was established between men and women, who were now given the right to vote. Once again the Japanese demonstrated their ability to change course and move rapidly in another direction.

Japan's economic recovery was slow at first. Most of the factories had been bombed during the war. Forests were stripped of their timber. It took time to get things started, but once launched the Japanese economy quickly took off. Less than twenty years after the end of World War II, the Japanese began enjoying renewed prosperity.

Today, everyone talks about Japan's GNP—gross national product, the total value of all goods and services produced by a nation within a specified time period. When you divide that figure by the total population, the result is the per capita GNP. After World War II, Japan's per capita GNP quickly soared. Not only was the country producing more goods and services, but because of an intentional slowdown in population growth, the total wealth was divided up among relatively fewer people. The United States became one of Japan's best customers, buying Canon cameras, Sony radios, Panasonic television sets, Honda motorcycles, and Toyota cars, as well as Japanese steel and other industrial goods. The boom continued for another twenty years, although recently some of that momentum has been lost.

As the value of the *yen*, the Japanese unit of currency, increases, the dollar buys fewer yen. This means that it takes more dollars to buy cars and television sets and cameras exported to the United States, where they are no longer such great bargains. American industry, resentful that Japan has been able to sell its products more cheaply than American-made products in the United States, now hopes to regain a bigger share of the market. Japanese investors, looking for places to put their money for a higher return than they can get at home, are buying American real estate, displaying a particular interest in famous skyscrapers and old landmarks. Japanese companies are opening factories in the United States and hiring American workers.

In the not-too-distant past, many Americans believed the Japanese were racially inferior and discriminated against them. During World War II, frightened Americans rounded up American-born people of Japanese ancestry and herded them into concentration camps, a clear example of racial prejudice. Today, many Japanese believe not only that they are Number One in terms of GNP and other measures of economic power, but that they are actually superior to *gaijin*, to anyone who is not Japanese—in fact, to the rest of the world.

It is not, of course, a question of who is superior to whom, of whose society works better, of whose students score higher on certain tests, of whose educational system is superior. It is a question of differences, and the differences between Japanese society and American society are many and deep.

2

Hammering Down the Nail

Aya and Midori

They look like typical Japanese schoolgirls in their shapeless blue jumpers and white shirts. But Aya's speech is totally American with a slight Bronx twang. She had been back in Japan from her vacation in New York for over a month when I met her, but her watch was still set on New York time.

I met Aya and her friend, Midori, in Tsukuba (TS'KOOH-bah) Science City, a community developed in 1972 by the Japanese government as a center for its scientific agencies. An hour's drive from Utsunomiya, Tsukuba is a rather gloomy place, marked by row after row of dreary government-owned apartment buildings and duplexes. Each building has a number, but even the locals have a hard time finding addresses.

Most of the men in Tsukuba are scientists who work for

21

the government. Many of them have gone overseas on research projects for several years at a time, taking their families with them. When the assignment ends and the family returns, there are adjustment problems, especially for the children. In a place like Tsukuba, the "returnee" is a common phenomenon.

Aya was three years old when her father, a biologist, took the family to New York City, ten when they returned to Japan. She's fourteen now, in the eighth grade. Last summer her parents took her and her younger sisters back to New York for a visit. "I really hated to leave," she said. "I cried and cried. New York is where I belong, with my real friends." Aya yearns for the day she will be old enough to go to college there to study interior design.

One of Aya's big problems when they first returned was learning to speak Japanese; she's still struggling to learn to read and write. Hers is an unusual family—both of her parents were eager to learn English and absorb American culture, and they spoke exclusively English to Aya and her sisters.

I asked Aya if her English teacher uses her as a resource, to help other students with their pronunciation. That was before I realized that Japanese students don't learn to *speak* English; the English they learn to read and write is grammatically stiff, using a somewhat outdated vocabulary. Aya said no; later I found out that it's hard enough on the teacher to have a student in the class whose English is so much better than the teacher's own.

"Lots of returnees pretend to speak English with a Japanese accent," Aya said. "That way people forget that they've been to America and they don't stick out."

Aya definitely sticks out. Unhappily she compared the unfriendly Japanese students in her present school to her friendly American classmates in New York. When Aya was growing up her mother explained to her that her face was different from an American face, that she was Japanese. But Aya thinks of herself as American: she's not interested in pretending to be Japanese.

Her younger sisters were both born in the United States. One had to repeat her year in nursery school when the family returned to Japan because she was too outgoing, had become too much of an individual. She hadn't absorbed the sense of being part of a group, and she didn't fit in. Aya says her sister hated returning to Japan, but she's younger and she's adapting. Aya isn't adapting. She doesn't want to, and the very fact that she has no desire to fit in shows how un-Japanese she really is.

Her friend Midori, also fourteen, had a different experience. She too spent most of her early years in the United States. Her family moved three times, and the constant relocation was hard on the family. When the children got older, Midori's mother brought them back to Japan while her father stayed in San Francisco; he'll be there for another year or so. During their time away, Midori's parents spoke Japanese to her, so there was less of a language problem. However, she is just as far behind as Aya in reading and writing. Despite the problems, Midori says she's glad to be back in Japan. She feels she belongs there. Aya doesn't.

Mrs. Murata dropped me off to stay with her acquaintance, Mrs. Yoshida, and her three children; Mrs. Yoshida's husband was out of town. A couple of years before, Mrs. Yoshida and the children—there were only two then—had gone with him to the United States for six months. He is now talking about returning for a longer stay, and she worries about the effect it will have on her children. Her son is nine now; if they all go in a year or so and stay for a couple of years, it might be very disruptive for him. She has seen

23

it happen to kids like Aya and Midori. That was one reason she invited them to come meet me.

"The nail that sticks up is hammered down"—so goes a saying quoted often in Japan, where society is highly organized and extremely rigid and where the individual who stands out is quickly pounded into conformity. But sometimes the hammering is not easy—sometimes the nail resists.

Japan has been described as a "vertical society" of many thin layers into which people are sorted according to a vast array of criteria, including sex, age, profession, status within that profession, and so on and on. In America, there are ways of measuring status, too, often connected with money, position, and power: the head of General Motors has more status than the owner of a garage. But we do not usually confer superior status on someone who graduated a year ahead of us in school, or who has been employed by a company a few years longer. In Japan, they do. We assume that status is equal between two friends or two business associates or a husband and wife. In Japan, they don't.

What's more, differences in status mean differences in the way the Japanese talk to each other, in the actual language they use, in how low they bow to one another. "Respect language" is hard to learn. The Japanese say you have to grow up in Japan in order to master it.

Japan is a society in which the group is *always* more important than the individual. People who assert their individuality are seen as selfish. Expressing an opinion is a symptom of individuality that could upset social harmony. The Japanese boy first learns about the group in his family. Then he is sent off to nursery school—or before that, to play school—to be "socialized," to learn to be part of the group. Like her brother, a Japanese girl is embarrassed to be singled out for attention. Japanese families encourage dependency; what we think of as "maturity" is much slower in coming. The Japanese measure maturity in terms of the individual's ability to behave according to the rules. The task of the child is to learn its place in that structure, to submit to the group. For those who learn the lesson well, life generally goes smoothly. For the rebel or the misfit, it's a different story.

This is the reverse of American society, where individualism—the more rugged the better—has always been treasured. In our families, we learn to be independent and self-reliant, to accept responsibility for ourselves as we grow up. In school, we are encouraged to think for ourselves.

Not so in Japan. The vast majority of Japanese teenagers have never lived abroad and experienced a different way of life; they don't think much about freedom, about being able to come and go and do as they please. They spend most of their days—long days—in school; most of their free time at home with their families, or with friends of the same sex. They don't go out on weeknights, except for extra tutoring at cram schools. They don't have cars (most ride bicycles to school, or take a train or bus). They don't date; they don't have friends of the opposite sex. And they don't notice the difference unless they've had another sort of experience in another country.

The girls from Utsunomiya Girls' High School who had been exchange students in the United States were away for only a year. They remembered the freedom they had seen in American high schools in Michigan, Minnesota, and Maryland, and spoke wistfully of how they missed that, how hard it had been to give up the freedom when they came back to all the stringent rules. A girl who had spent a year in Mexico had a different problem: although Mexican schools are conservative, not too different in philosophy from Japan's, the personality of the people is radically different. This girl had enjoyed the bright colors of the clothes and houses, and the emotional openness of the Mexican people. When she returned home and began to express her feelings freely, as she had been encouraged to do in Mexico, she quickly learned that to do so was "not Japanese."

Most Americans view the opportunity to travel abroad, to live and study in another culture for a year or two, as a highly desirable experience, giving lucky students a broader understanding of the world. Not all Japanese are so sure of the benefits. Some see such travel as a crippling interruption in the rigidly programmed course of study in high school: missing a year might mean never catching up, never regaining the edge necessary to place well in the university entrance exams.

Others worry that impressionable young people will pick up "American color," become too much influenced by the foreign culture, and bring home ideas that don't work in Japan. Students who have learned to raise their hands in class, to volunteer answers, to ask questions, and to offer opinions learn quickly that this is considered "too American" and inappropriate.

There are now about forty thousand Japanese kids living abroad, most of them with their families and about 60 percent in the U.S. Each year some ten thousand return to Japan and struggle with reentry. One problem they face is having fallen behind in their schoolwork, even though some were able to attend one of the three full-time Japanese schools in New York, Chicago, or Los Angeles. Others go to special Saturday cram schools, in an attempt at least to keep up Japanese language skills. But more important than the academic problems are the psychological ones, especially when teachers and other students give the returnees a hard time for being "different."

Takeo

He bowed formally when we met and sat at rigid attention while I tried to talk to him. Takeo, thirteen, had recently returned to Japan after living in the United States for ten years. For all those years, his parents had worked hard to give him a typical Japanese upbringing; for the last two he had attended a Japanese school in New York. His parents taught him respect language—how to discern the layers of Japanese society and how to behave accordingly.

The head English teacher of the junior high school told me about Takeo and asked if I wanted to meet him; of course I did. What I hoped for was fifteen or twenty minutes alone with him where, with some luck, he might tell me how he felt about coming "back" to a place he didn't remember at all and where the expectations were so radically different.

What I got, though, was a formal meeting in the principal's office with Takeo, the English teacher, an American teacher, and even a kid visiting from New Zealand for a few days—presumably because we all spoke English. There was no time alone with Takeo, no chance to talk about what it was really like to come back, about how he really felt.

Instead we dealt with data—Takeo's age, how long he had lived in the U.S., what the major problems were in returning. Takeo said, stiffly, that he was having a hard time catching up with his written Japanese. Two years of Japanese schooling in New York hadn't been enough to make up for all he had missed.

It was the American teacher who told me later about Takeo's main problem: he was too "Japanese-y." For years his parents had struggled to inculcate him thoroughly with proper Japanese behavior. The trouble was, it was *their* behavior—the behavior of another generation. Kids didn't act that way anymore, and to students his own age, Takeo seemed laughably quaint and old-fashioned. In subtle ways Takeo was different, although those subtleties, like being just a shade too polite, would not be apparent to non-Japanese. Close, but not close enough. Takeo stuck out. Maybe he too would get hammered down before it was too late.

Masao

It's too late for Masao. "I'm just a typical Japanese, Ms. Meyer," he said, pronouncing it MY-ah, and I resisted contradicting him. Masao speaks with an elegant British accent, and the clipped tones seem incongruous in the mouth of this terribly serious young Japanese. Masao is twenty-four. His father is a banker, and when Masao was nine years old, the family moved to London for three years. Those three years were especially cruel to Masao; he knew how to speak perfect English, but at the age of twelve hadn't learned what it was to be Japanese. When he returned to Japan, he was a total misfit. The nail stuck up sharply; the harder it was pounded, the more fiercely it seemed to resist.

Masao dropped out of school for several years, isolating himself from his peers and eliminating any possibility that he would learn to fit in. Obviously extremely bright, he studied at home for seven years, suffering all that time from what he still sees as his great failure: to behave like a proper Japanese, to become part of the group. He passed the entrance examinations for a private university in Tokyo noted for its studies in the literature of other languages. Now he's a graduate student at Tsukuba University.

We were introduced by Mrs. Murata, who, at the age of 52, was working on a doctorate at the same university and shares an office with Masao. We went to the university dining hall for lunch. Masao wasn't interested in eating; he looked at my bowl of noodles and commented that he had been used to eating much better food when he lived in Tokyo.

"I'd be happy to help you in whatever way I can, Ms. Meyer," he said. "Please feel free to ask me questions."

But I didn't feel free. The questions I wanted to ask him were too hard: Why did you drop out of school when you came back? Exactly what happened to you? What did the students do to you to make life so unbearable? But the look on his face was too painful; he seemed tense, anxious, under a great deal of stress. Slurping noodles in a noisy cafeteria didn't seem like the right setting for such probing, personal questions.

So we danced around the subject. "What are your goals?" I asked, offering something I thought safe.

"To be a perfect Japanese," he said.

"What does that mean?"

"To conform perfectly, to fit in perfectly with Japanese society."

"Why is that important?"

"Because it's a sign of maturity."

"In America it's a sign of maturity to accept yourself, to acknowledge that you are different and that you can't ever live up to a model of perfection," I said.

"I can never stop trying," he said.

"Would you consider going back to England to live for a while? Or to the United States?"

"No."

After Masao left for a class, his office-mate and I looked at each other. "What do you think?" she asked.

"I think he's got real problems," I said. "At home we'd call it an identity crisis and send him to a psychologist."

"He's having a hard time," she said. "He doesn't relate

well to his professors. He can never quite figure out what he's supposed to do—when he should stand up and when it's all right to stay seated, when he should bow and how low, when he should offer to make the tea. Everything is a struggle for him. He makes mistakes and feels humiliated. He's very much aware of his failure—to himself, to his family, to his culture. He's an outsider, and that's the worst thing you can be in Japan."

More Returnees

The next day I met some women who had gone abroad with their husbands and then come home again. Their experiences were as varied as the children's had been. It seemed that different personalities reacted in different ways; some people were more adaptable than others.

Some women complained that other wives regarded them as "different" and shunned them. But there were many such returnees in Tsukuba Science City, and they seemed to stick together. Those who went abroad with good English skills usually had a good time; those who didn't, learned. One woman had spent two years with her husband at Pennsylvania State University, thirty miles from my hometown in rural Pennsylvania. For two years she had traveled throughout the countryside, going to auctions and farm sales; on weekends the whole family had taken short trips. I experienced a moment of disorientation when I walked into her home, decorated with Pennsylvania Dutch quilts and antiques, the kinds of things I grew up with.

For some women, the return had presented practical problems: prices had shot up while they were away. And some had to deal with taking care of children alone, while the husband remained behind in the U.S. or some other place for a year or so. This is apparently not as difficult a situation for a Japanese wife as it would be for an American. "You must learn these words," one Japanese wife said to me, spelling them out: *tanshin funin*. They refer to the man who lives apart from his family, who stays at home when his company sends him off to work somewhere else. It's not unusual for Japanese husbands to be away from their families for long periods, either in foreign countries or in other parts of Japan.

Although there are problems for returnees, both children and adults, most mothers I met were trying to make the trip abroad a positive experience for their children and worked hard to keep up the children's foreign language skills. Some kids go to the Bunko Association, a library for children who have lived overseas for at least a year and whose parents want them to keep up their foreign language skills.

Mrs. Yoshida takes her nine-year-old son to English conversation class one evening a week. There's a chain of some twenty classrooms sprinkled around Tsukuba. The boy's teacher happens to be that most prized of English teachers in Japan, a native speaker. Joseph is a tall, blond man in his mid-twenties who is a real oddity: he's "BIJ," born in Japan, which is why I couldn't place a regional American accent—he doesn't have any. He plays games like Simon Says and strums his guitar to accompany such typical American songs as "Carry Me Back to Old Virginny" and "Oh, Susannah!"

Although the children in his class spoke pretty good English, I wondered aloud if they knew what they were singing—especially the contradictions of raining in dry weather and freezing in hot sunshine. And how did he explain "old darky?" ("Ol' Massah" had mercifully been changed to something else.) "I don't," Joseph said.

When they sang about the prairie moon that is "Deep in the Heart of Texas," I sang along with them, clapping in rhythm.

3

Language and Writing: The Heart of Japanese Culture

Speaking "the Devil's Language"

Good morning	*ohayo gozaimasu* (OH-hy-oh goh-zy-mahss)
Good afternoon	*konnichi-wa* (KOHN-nee-chee-wah)
Good evening	*komban-wa* (KOHM-bahn-wah)
Pardon me	*sumimasen* (SOO-mee-mah-sen)
Please	*dozo* (DOH-zoh)
Thank you	*domo arigato* (DOH-moh ah-ree-gah-toh)
Yes	*hai* (HY)
No	*iie* (EE-eh)
Good-bye	*sayonara* (SAH-yoh-nah-rah)

I made no attempt to learn Japanese before my trip, partly because I knew any real command of the language would take years to acquire, and partly because I had learned from experience that knowing "a little" often creates more problems than it solves. Instead I settled for a handful of polite phrases.

Nihongo is the Japanese word for the Japanese language. As languages go, *Nihongo* is not hard to learn to pronounce. It has a simple phonetic system—there are only fourteen consonants, and the vowel sounds are much like Spanish or Italian:

a = like the *a* in *father*
e = like the *e* in *pet*
i = like the *i* in *machine*
o = like the *o* in *home*
u = like the *u* in *rude*
ai = like the *i* in *high*
ei = like the *ay* in *pay*

Most Japanese consonants sound like the English equivalent, although the *r* is softly rolled, like an Englishman saying "veddy nice day." The *f* is formed without placing the teeth against the lower lip; it sounds more like a *wh*, as in *who*. And sometimes *u* and *i* aren't vocalized—they're "whispered," or dropped altogether. The familiar word *futon* turned out not to be pronounced the way I'd always said it, FOOH-tahn, but rather, wh'-TOHN.

Compared to English, *Nihongo* is an unstressed language with slight emphasis on the first syllable, the rest pronounced evenly. (English speakers tend to put stress on the next-to-last syllable, as in Spanish or Italian.) When I first met Masako, a Japanese student at the University of New Mexico, I pronounced her name mah-SAH-koh, and she went along with the mispronunciation. By the time I visited her in Japan, I had learned to pronounce it correctly: MAH-sah-koh.

Japanese uses long and short vowels, sometimes writing

34

them (in the Roman alphabet) as a double vowel or with a long mark over the vowel. The man's name *Shuuichi*, for example, is also written *Shūichi*. Doubling the letter or a long mark doesn't change the sound of the letter, only the slight difference in length: *Shūichi* is pronounced SHOOOO-ee-chee, rather than SHOO-ee-chee.

The simplicity of the Japanese language ends with its pronunciation. Japanese is so complex and so different from almost all other languages that it was referred to as "the Devil's language" by Francis Xavier, the sixteenth-century Jesuit missionary. The Germanic languages (which include English), Romance languages (such as Spanish, Italian, and French), and several other subgroups all belong to the Indo-European family of languages, the most widespread of the language families. Chinese, part of the Sinitic family, has little in common with any Indo-European language—or with Japanese, which uses the same writing system. Chinese, like English, depends heavily on word order in a sentence for its meaning; Japanese does not. *Nihongo* does not belong to a large family of languages, although there are a few other languages it seems to be related to, like Mongolian and Korean.

The Japanese language tends to leave a lot unspoken. There is no singular or plural; it doesn't have the feminine and masculine genders of Spanish and other Romance languages; it doesn't have the articles *a* and *the*. Speakers don't use the subject of a sentence if it can be determined by the context or some other clues. "Foreigners speaking Japanese always say too much," one Japanese woman told me. "They put too many words in a sentence. We leave them out."

Japanese is a "respect language" with infinite subtle—and sometimes not so subtle—differences in the way people talk to each other: women speak one way, men another; children address their parents and teachers quite differently from the way adults address their elders and their children. My friend Masako says that when she came to the United States, she was amazed to discover that people use exactly the same language no matter whom they were talking to.

Japanese is also a rapidly changing language. It originally borrowed heavily from the Chinese, but as Japan became involved in the international community, words began to come into the language from other sources. One of the principal sources, was—and is—English; the list of English words that have come into the language goes on and on. The Japanese are skilled at absorbing new vocabulary from other languages and adapting it to their own more limited range of sounds. Most of these words are as unrecognizable to a speaker of English as ancient Japanese. I met an American teacher who lived and worked for years in Japan and is perfectly fluent in the language, but who must go back once a year to keep up with the borrowings. He described a lecture he had attended where he kept hearing the word *kone*, a word he didn't recognize. When the lecture ended, he asked a Japanese colleague what it meant. The colleague was amazed that he didn't know it—after all, it was an English word! Finally they worked it out: *kone* was the first part of the word *connection;* the Japanese had retained only that part and discarded the rest.

And what was I to make of a suggestion that I eat at *Makudonarudo?* That turned out to be "McDonald's." The Japanese stick a vowel in between each pair of consonants because their language doesn't have "consonant clusters," like the *rd* in *card,* the *lt* in *melt,* or the *lk* in *milk.* They pronounce an English word their way, and we can't understand it.

Writing "the Devil's Language"

Language is not the same thing as writing. Language is a system of communicating by vocal symbols, and human beings have been making noises at each other since the origin of the species. But according to most experts, *writing*, the visible recording of language, is a fairly recent development, dating back about eight thousand years. Most writing is *phonemic*, attempting to symbolize all the significant sounds of the language; the result is an alphabet. Speakers of English and other languages of Western Europe write with the Roman alphabet, which is derived from the Greek (which in turn came from the Phoenicians).

But not all languages are written phonetically, or according to sound. Both Chinese and Japanese use thousands of characters that are not equivalent in any way to the sounds of their languages. In Chinese, each character symbolizes a word or concept. Chinese characters were originally fairly simple pictographs; today there are thousands of them, each representing a one-syllable Chinese word.

For a long time, there was no written Japanese. From the sixth through the ninth centuries, when the Japanese were copying and borrowing as much as they could from the Chinese, they were also learning to read and write Chinese. Then the Japanese developed a phonetic system called *kana*, in which each character stands for a syllable, like *ka* and *na* (in the alphabet system, each character stands for an individual *sound*, like *k, a,* and *n*). This system is called a *syllabary*, and the Japanese language has two of them, each with forty-eight characters: *katakana* is used for foreign words; *hiragana* for everything else.

In the tenth and eleventh centuries, the Japanese were writing their literature in *kana*. At the same time, they were taking more and more Chinese characters into their lan-

37

guage. But the simple Japanese phonetic system altered the way many adopted Chinese characters were pronounced, oversimplifying them. As a result, perhaps a hundred entirely different Chinese characters will have the exact same pronunciation in Japanese. On the other hand, a single character may have several different meanings as well as pronunciations.

Eventually, after hundreds of years, the Japanese written language emerged as a combination of thousands of Chinese characters, called *kanji*, and the two *kana* syllabaries. The result is probably the most complex and difficult system of writing used in the world today. It's a system that requires an enormous amount of rote memorization just to be able to read a newspaper.

Although an unabridged Japanese dictionary contains more than 50,000 characters (some made up of forty separate strokes), students need memorize "only" some 2,000 *kanji*, many of which can be read or pronounced in several ways. Much of what a Japanese child does in school is learn to read and write. A first grader masters 76 *kanji* characters, plus the two syllabaries; a second grader learns 145 characters; a third grader, 195 characters; and so on at the rate of about 200 characters a year, through nine years of compulsory education. At the end of nine years of such intensive study, the student can read a newspaper but not a college textbook or serious literature.

Kanji and *kana* are combined according to certain rules to form words and sentences. The *kana* are clear in their pronunciation, but the Chinese characters almost always can be pronounced several different ways. Individual words are not separated from each other, and children learning to read have to figure out which symbols to group together to form a word. Japanese is read vertically, from top to bottom, starting with the column on the right. Japanese newspapers, and most books, are printed that way; science and arithmetic, however are written and read horizontally, from left to right like English. Children must learn both styles. The sheer amount of material to be memorized seems overwhelming, and yet Japan has succeeded in producing an astoundingly high literacy rate: *98 percent* of all Japanese can read and write at a ninth-grade level, and furthermore, they do. Most people read at least one newspaper a day, and Japan is said to be a nation of bookworms—people haunt bookstores.

Some Japanese (and many non-Japanese) wonder if there mightn't be a simpler way to write *Nihongo*. Chinese characters don't suit the Japanese language any more than they suit English or German. Why invest so much time and energy memorizing thousands of characters that bear no relation to the sound of the words? Neither *katakana* nor *hiragana* has the necessary phonetic flexibility. However, some people think *romaji*, the Roman alphabet, would work well; according to one scholar, it's possible to write Japanese perfectly with only nineteen Roman letters.

Sensible as it seems, not many people are seriously interested in the idea. One reason is that those who have worked very hard to master something as difficult as *kanji* don't like to think there's any other way to do it. Opponents say no one would be able to read the great literature unless it were translated. And, of course, *kanji* is deeply embedded in the culture; it's part of being Japanese. The fact that their writing is so difficult and generally inaccessible to the outside world is valued by the Japanese, who cherish a sense of their own specialness, perhaps of their own superiority. Such attitudes don't change easily, even when the changes make perfectly good sense to *gaijin*.

Japanese writing emphasizes the correct formation of each character—there is no room for sloppiness or individuality. Children begin formal training in calligraphy, using traditional brushes and ink, in third grade. One afternoon I visited a private calligraphy class, where several eight- or nine-year-olds knelt at low tables, hunched over sheets of white paper divided into large squares. Each child held a brush and, carefully copying a sample, made the same character over and over, one per square.

The calligraphy master, a good-humored man in a blue work shirt wrapped and tied at his waist, beckoned me over to his table. He poured water into the well of an ink block and mixed it with an ink stick. Next, he dipped a fat brush into the ink and rolled the tip to a fine point. Then, on one thin soft sheet of paper at a time, he made a series of six characters. *Ai*, the character for love, was fairly complicated, but the rest were simple, representing water, river, tree, grove (two tree symbols), and forest (three trees).

Then it was my turn. He showed me how to hold my arm parallel to the table, how to dip the brush and shape the tip, how to place the character on the paper with large, firm strokes. My giant-size samples, one per page, were not nearly as neat as the children's and could not be compared to the master's own framed examples, tiny characters exquisitely rendered in fine brush strokes.

Until recently all writing in Japan was done by hand, but now there are special word processors for *kanji*. Unlike most American word processors, which are software programs operated by personal computers, the Japanese machines are like electronic typewriters. A writer explained to me how she uses hers. First she types the word she wants to use in *romaji* and presses a button; the machine then scrolls a list of all the Chinese characters represented by that phonetic spelling. She chooses the appropriate character and presses another button, entering her selection. It's an incredibly slow process compared to an American word processor (or even to a typewriter with our twenty-six letters), but, as she said, "It makes an unbearably slow task at least bearably slow."

Learning English

Considering how difficult it is for the Japanese to learn to write their own language, it would seem that learning English ought to be a snap. It isn't—at least, not when it comes to speaking it. The same profound linguistic differences that make learning to speak Japanese so hard for an American also work in reverse.

Nevertheless, the Japanese are intent on becoming a bilingual country with English as the second language. So far, this plan has been a massive failure. All students are required to study English through three years of junior high school, when compulsory education ends. Most students continue on through high school; by the time they graduate they've endured six years of instruction in the English language. Yet scarcely any Japanese can speak more than a few words (although they're supposedly better at reading).

When people asked me what I thought of their English instruction, I was frank with them. I said I thought it was useless, but I wasn't telling them anything they didn't already know: instruction starts too late and relies too heavily on textbooks.

Unfortunately, English teaching in Japan is geared to the university entrance exams. This means that proficiency in English has nothing to do with speaking or understanding, but everything to do with how students answer the multiple-choice questions, mostly based on archaic vocabulary and obscure grammatical constructions. My revolutionary (to them) idea, passed along to teachers and students who asked me, was that English be taken off the entrance exams and taught as a living means of communication, starting in first grade.

One teacher who was still struggling with English told me Japanese educators joke that most Americans can't pass the English examination. I would love to have tried, but I suspect he is probably right—I would have flunked it cold. But my conclusions are not the same as his. The Japanese see the failure of Americans as a weakness of our educational system. I agree that we often fail to educate our children to read and write well, but I think the joke is really on the Japanese: even if I flunk their tricky written test, I can speak English; I can communicate. They can't.

Most Japanese teachers of English can't speak well because they've never heard English spoken properly. They've been taught by Japanese teachers; only a few have learned from native speakers, and fewer still have studied in the U.S. or Great Britain. The Ministry of Education is trying to correct this by sending Japanese teachers to America and England and bringing American teachers to work in Japan. But as long as the emphasis focuses on reading and writing, not much will change. People who want to learn to speak English for business or personal use must either attend special language classes or find tutors.

Studying English is fashionable in Japan: there are schools and teachers everywhere (of varying degrees of quality), as well as instructional programs on NHK, Japanese public television. I tuned in to NHK one evening and watched a drill on comparatives ("I am *taller* than my father"), a section on phonetics (the *u* in *uniform* and *run*), and a reading exercise: "Softball is a game very like baseball. It started in the United States in 1895. . . ." and so on, a little sports history. It's American, not British, English that they want to speak. But what American says "very like"?

An American friend who teaches English to Japanese business people told me that the Japanese understand each other when they speak English because they all mispronounce things in the same way—saying an *r* for an *l*, and a *z* instead of a *th*. I sat in on one of his classes and watched him work with his students on accurate pronunciation. He drew a diagram on the blackboard showing them exactly how to put the upper teeth against the lower lip to make an *f* sound. He sympathized with their struggle to say a word like *strengths*, with eight consonants and one vowel. He led them through exercises on the difference between *in*, *on*, and *at*. He explained our habit of using tag questions, with the subtle differences between "You're going, aren't you?" and "You're not going, are you?" His students worked hard to follow his instructions and absorb the material.

One of this teacher's pet gripes is the English textbooks written by Japanese who insist on making English an overly polite language by including phrases like "Please allow me to introduce myself." "That's something you might say if you were meeting the president of the United States," he said. "In most situations, you would simply say, 'Hello, my name is ———.' "

Given all the peculiarities of pronunciation, I usually had to struggle to get past Japanese accents, even when the speaker was fairly fluent. One college student with a good vocabulary always substituted a *w* for both *r* and *l*. Sometimes it was just frustrating, but occasionally it was funny.

I was sightseeing in Kyoto with a friend of a friend, a Japanese woman in her early thirties who had majored in English in college. Kyoto is a beautiful city where walking is a pleasure, and we had been walking and talking for hours. Both of us were exhausted, but neither of us wanted to admit that we had had enough. Finally we stopped at a coffee shop for a snack and a chance to rest.

"Do you want to walk some more?" Mrs. Koyama asked me, "or would you rather take a *bass*?"

At least it sounded like "bass," and having learned that

Japanese usually substitute an *s* or a *z* for the *th* sound of English, I thought she said "bath." One of the great traditions of Japan is the public bath, and so far I had missed it. I had wanted to experience it, but knowing there was probably an elaborate protocol, a code of conduct, I didn't want to try it by myself and do something gauche. Now here was this woman suggesting a way to recuperate from our miles of walking. The idea of sinking my weary bones into a tub of hot water sounded very appealing.

"That's a wonderful idea," I said, relaxing over my English tea. But then I began to think about it, and I had questions.

"I've never done it before," I confessed.

"I'll go with you," she said.

"Is it nearby?" I asked.

"There are many near here."

Time passed; we talked about other things, but the bath was still on my mind. I said, "I'm really looking forward to being in hot water up to my nose." She smiled. Finally I asked my ultimate question: "Do men and women take them together?"

This time she stared at me blankly, and in that split second I saw my mistake: we were taking a *bus*, not a bath. Her mispronunciation was of the vowel, not the consonants.

The Japanese are in love with English. They use it in their advertising, print it all over their clothes, use it to name their restaurants and shops, and decorate all sorts of items with it—apparently without checking with a native speaker for accuracy. The results are often hilarious.

Given their problems pronouncing certain sounds, I could not figure out why the Japanese persisted in giving their cars unpronounceable model names like *Corolla*, *Bluebird*, *Laurel*, and *Langley*. The explanation someone offered was that the *r* sound in Japanese connotes speed and power, and since an *l* is pronounced like an *r*, they can pack a lot of power into one model name.

Americans collect some of the wackier examples of "Japanese English" and swap stories. One English-language magazine runs a column called "Funny English" and pays a thousand yen (about seven dollars) for items submitted by watchful readers. One winner was a Tokyo bar named Wet Dream. Another was a candy bar called Almond Torrid Bit Chocolate, with this appeal to the buyer: "Nuts have never been this happy with chocolate. Taste their love in every bite."

One day I saw a little boy in Dunkin' Donuts wearing a T-shirt with this message: ADVANCE SPORT SPIRIT. MAKING YOURSELF CONDITION POWERFUL WITH THE ALL YOUR STRENGTH. Now what is a speaker of English to make of that? The spelling is fine. The grammar is—well, a little odd, to say the least.

I have on my desk a totally useless souvenir, a wooden plaque inscribed with various English phrases. I got it because it makes absolutely no sense. SEXY SUMMER it says in capital letters, then: "She has become coquettish lately in summer. That girl is too exciting for us. So we like summer best!" The punchline: I HAVE A LONGING FOR THE BIG WEDNESDAY.

4

Religion and Tradition: What the Japanese Believe

Maiko-chan and Mr. Shirota

Maiko is small-boned and delicate, like most Japanese women. She had on sandals and a round straw hat with a narrow brim and ribbons, like those worn by little girls. She looked very young. I nearly always underestimated the age of the Japanese I met, especially young people. I would have guessed Maiko was about twelve, but in fact she was nineteen. *Chan* is the diminutive form of address for children and young people, and I began to call her Maiko-chan as an affectionate name.

I met Maiko for the first time at the airport, waiting with her bunch of roses and her welcome sign. A few days later she invited me to spend a day sightseeing with her in Kamakura, where she lives, a pretty town famous for its shrines and temples. Maiko's father, an executive with Sony, makes the two-hour commute to work in downtown Tokyo;

46

Maiko makes the same trip to the university where she is studying English literature.

When she was twelve, Maiko's father was transferred to San Diego, and she and her younger brother went to school there for five years. Maiko graduated from high school in California, but she never felt comfortable there. "I was very shy," she said. "Americans are very outgoing. Of course I had a hard time learning English. Everyone was kind. But it was too hard for me. I was a serious schoolgirl."

"Would you have been a serious schoolgirl if you had been here in Japan?" I asked.

"No," she said and giggled, covering her mouth with her hand, as Japanese women do when they laugh.

Getting to Kamakura from downtown Tokyo was complicated, involving two subways to Yokohama and a local train from there. I was frankly nervous about the venture, but determined to try. Against incredible odds, I ran into Mr. Shirota in the huge Yokohama train station. He was on his way to meet Maiko, too. Although Mr. Shirota is a graduate student who teaches English, conversation between us was always strained, and he left most of the talking to Maiko. Both were willing and tireless tour guides, eager to show me whatever there was to see. But I had to go back to my reading to understand what it is that the Japanese believe.

Shinto, Buddhism, and Confucianism

Shrines and temples in tourist centers like Kamakura are what is left of Japan's ancient splendor, much of it destroyed by earthquakes and war and the relentless expansion of a population that has run out of space for homes and factories. Amid boring miles of cement block and concrete are occasional picturesque oases like Kamakura, the Old Japan that tourists hope to see. Preserved in its quiet beauty are expressions of the religious tradition and philosophical thought that shape the Japanese worldview.

Through the centuries three distinct patterns have been woven into the picture Japanese have of themselves in the cosmos. The first and oldest religion, Shinto, provided a sense of awe at the world of nature, plus a vibrant collection of celebrations and customs. The second, Buddhism, introduced a mystical dimension that transcends the natural world. The third, Confucianism, contributed a system of ethical behavior.

The ancient religion of Japan, once centered around the worship of gods called *kami,* came to be called Shinto, meaning "the way of the gods." The early Japanese found their gods in natural phenomena like the sun and moon, mountains and rivers, rocks and trees. They also worshiped mythological ancestors, like the sun goddess, from whom their emperors claimed descent.

As it's practiced today, Shinto focuses on pilgrimages to famous shrines, celebrations and festivals, and ritual observances. Ceremonial purity and physical cleanliness are extremely important; some think that's why the Japanese place so much emphasis on bathing and make a distinction between clean house slippers and dirty outside shoes. Shinto is a simple, uncomplicated religion. It doesn't involve concepts of right and wrong or a belief in life after death, as do other major religions of the world.

In the sixth century a new and quite different religion began to filter into Japan from China, along with many other cultural influences. Buddhism, a highly mystical religion, is concerned with the salvation of each individual soul through meditation and self-discipline. Contrasted with the simplicity of Shinto, Buddhism has a complex philosphy. Gradually it became the dominant religion, as important to Japan as Christianity was to the West. Shinto didn't disappear, nor was it absorbed into Buddhism. The two simply coexisted.

After the Meiji Restoration in 1868, emphasis on old-time Shinto was revived. It became the state religion, and, removed from its roots in nature and redefined as patriotism and nationalistic fervor, was used by the militarists to explain and glorify their policy of aggression. After World War II, Shinto didn't disappear then, either; it continued as a matter of custom. The Japanese see no contradiction in practicing Shinto and Buddhism simultaneously. The two are comfortably separate in the Japanese mind: Shinto for festivals and ceremonies celebrating birth and events in the lives of the young; Buddhism when death draws near and there is concern for the soul of the departed. On O-Bon (All Souls) in August, people return to their hometowns to honor the dead, and during the weeks of spring and fall equinoxes, there are special Buddhist services. Almost everyone in Japan claims affiliation with one of the Buddhist sects or with some kind of religion, but the number of people with strong religious ties has dropped. Few young people today practice a religion.

There are Buddhist monasteries and temples and Shinto shrines all over Japan, in rural areas and sometimes right in the middle of bustling business districts. Shrines are recognizable by the *torii*, the gateway made of two upright pillars with two crosspieces. The *torii* is always painted red, an important color in Japan. The great bronze temple bells are struck with a wooden log each morning at six and again at six in the evening. Children play in the gardens of the temples and shrines, sometimes the only open space or spot of greenery in a neighborhood. Most funerals are conducted by Buddhist priests; the dead are cremated, their ashes buried in cemeteries crowded with stone obelisks.

Beginning in the seventeeth century, the ideas of the Chinese philosopher Confucius began to have an impact on Japan. Confucianism is not a religious belief with a traditional form of worship; rather, it is an ethical system that stresses rational order and emphasizes loyalty, personal relationships, and standards of behavior. Confucianism places importance on education and hard work. At the time of Confucius, China was a male-dominated society in which the woman's role was strictly to bear children and care for the family; that value persists, although it is changing. Confucianism has more influence than either Shinto or Buddhism on the way Japanese people think and behave.

Visiting the Shrines

Mr. Shirota, who is in his mid-twenties, says young Japanese are not religious—except in the spring around entrance examination time, when senior high school students flock to the shrine of the deity of learning and write their names and the names of the schools they want to enter on a small wooden plaque.

Mr. Shirota's parents say prayers every day at the little "ancestor shelf" in their home, but he does not. Yet as we approached a Shinto shrine in Kamakura, Mr. Shirota and Maiko both stopped at a well with long-handled dippers. This was for purification, they said. They dipped up water and poured it over one hand, then the other; slurped up some water from their cupped hands to purify their mouths; swished the water around; then spit it out on the ground. It was a ritual we observed at each shrine we visited that day. And at every shrine Mr. Shirota clapped his hands twice "to call down the gods," placed the palms of his hands together and bowed his head, then tossed several coins into the boxes nearby.

On trees near the shrines twists of white paper fluttered like leaves on branches and twigs. Maiko said they were fortunes people had purchased at the shrine. "If you don't like your fortune, you fold it and tie it on the tree. That can improve your luck." I paid a hundred yen (about seventy cents) to a vendor who handed me a wooden box. I shook out a long stick with a number, indicating the cubbyhole from which to take a slip of paper. Maiko studied my fortune.

"It's a good fortune," she said. " 'Whatever project you're working on now should go very well. Success is assured.' " There was other information on health and marriage, all good. I didn't need to tie my slip to a tree.

At the entrance to a shrine honoring Hachiman, the god of war, is the Drum Bridge, a half cylinder so steep—and so slippery—that you can't walk over it. I watched some determined people hauling themselves up one side and down the other by a handrail, also slippery. Maiko said crossing the bridge grants easy delivery in childbirth; I suspect that any woman strong enough to drag herself over that bridge would probably have an easy delivery anyway.

At the money-washing shrine we emptied all our coins into wicker baskets and swished them around in water to purify them. Thinking we were supposed to leave the coins behind as a donation, I was stingy with mine. Then I found out that whatever you wash is supposed to be returned to you many times—you don't gamble a thing. I was immediately sorry I hadn't washed every yen I had. This was the first week of my trip, and I was in a constant panic that I would run out of money. The dollar was worth about ¥140, only half as many as a year or so before. I had discovered that a cup of coffee or English tea cost at least ¥300, and when I picked up the tab for our three soft drinks that afternoon, it cost over ten dollars.

After a while the temples and shrines began to look alike to me, but there were two stunning exceptions. One was Daibutsu, an enormous bronze Buddha thirty-six feet high that has gazed serenely through half-closed eyes over the city of Kamakura for more than seven hundred years.

The other was the sight of hundreds and hundreds of little wooden statues no more than six inches high, many of them wearing little crocheted berets or key chains with good-luck charms. They are images of Jizo, the Buddhist patron of babies, dedicated to the safety of the souls of dead babies and aborted fetuses. (Abortion is common in Japan, the customary way women deal with unwanted pregnancies.) Buddhist temples are sometimes surrounded with entire fields of the little statues.

Before we left that temple, we entered a small shelter called the *Kyozo*, where all the Buddhist scriptures are stored. In the center of the *Kyozo* is a pillar with all the scriptures on shelves that revolve around it. Turning the huge cylinder is the equivalent of reading all the prayers. Maiko and Mr. Shirota cooperated to turn it once.

When babies are about a month old, they're taken to the shrine to receive special blessings and, sometimes, a name. I stayed for a couple of days with a family that had taken both their sons to the shrine and been given traditional names for them. The elder son was named Takebumi, a combination of *take*, meaning sword, and *bumi*, meaning pen. His younger brother's name, Yukimasa, combines *yuki*, happiness, and *masa*, growth or prosperity. *Masa* is a favorite name, often with an *o* ending for boys—Masao (MAH-sah-oh)—and a *ko* ending for girls—Masako (MAH-sah-koh). When I was first learning Japanese names, I had no way of distinguishing masculine from feminine. Then someone gave me a clue: if the name ends in *ko*, it's always a girl; about 60 percent of all female names end in *ko*.

One of the most popular Shinto celebrations is observed nationally on November 15. It's called the 7-5-3 Celebration, and on that day boys aged three and five and girls aged three and seven are dressed up—the little girls often in *kimono*, the boys usually in Western-style dress suits—and taken to shrines for rites for the children's protection and prayers for good fortune.

Twenty is the year young Japanese come of age, and the event is celebrated not at individual birthday parties, but at a big public party held on January 15 for everyone who turned twenty that year. Japanese girls wear beautiful kimonos for the event. Most women wear the long-sleeved robe—usually made of rich silk, with an *obi*, a wide sash—only for dress-up occasions. There are always a few elderly women out shopping and riding the subway in kimonos, but a young woman in a kimono is usually on her way to some special occasion.

I asked Mrs. Koyama, the woman with whom I had taken a bus, if she often wore a kimono. "I can't wear it by myself," she said. At first I thought she meant that unescorted ladies did not appear in public in a kimono, but I had seen dozens of them, so I knew that couldn't be it. Then I realized she had meant "can't put it on" rather than "can't wear it." It requires help to arrange the gown and long, heavy sash, but some manufacturers are adjusting to the times and marketing nontraditional kimonos that are easy for women to put on without anyone's help. These kimonos are sold in stylish boutiques and worn to nightclubs by a new generation of young women with plenty of money to spend.

One day I browsed through Mitsukoshi, a huge department store in the Ginza, Tokyo's famous shopping district. I rode the escalators from the main floor to the top and back down through several subbasements, thinking that it didn't look much different from any U.S. department store—until I stumbled upon the kimono department. Set apart from the others, it was carpeted with traditional straw mats; and customers as well as sales clerks padded around without shoes. Two sales clerks hovered over a girl being fitted in a gorgeous blue silk kimono with wide, loose sleeves that came almost to the floor. The women draped the robe over her denim skirt and shirt and arranged a broad obi around her middle, transforming her in seconds from a pretty teen-age girl into a traditionally elegant Japanese lady while her mother and grandmother knelt nearby, smiling approval.

On May 5, the fifth day of the fifth month, the whole country celebrates Children's Day as a national holiday, closing schools and offices. It was originally a festival for boys, and families with sons would fly streamers in the form of a carp outside the house. The carp is the symbol for boys because it supposedly swims against the current, showing strength in adversity. Inside the house warrior dolls are put on display.

The third day of the third month used to be the festival for the girls, but now that the two are combined in May, March 3 is the Doll Festival. Some people display elaborately dressed dolls representing the emperor, empress, and so on. Costumed dolls seem to be a favorite collector's item on permanent exhibit in many Japanese homes. One family I visited keeps the son's warrior doll and badminton racquets decorated with costume dolls belonging to the two girls in the tokonoma, the alcove that is part of the traditional Japanese room.

New Year's is the big festival in Japan; most people visit a Shinto shrine on that day, and it's an occasion for partying and celebration as well as for exchanging gifts. Some families who like to do things Western-style also observe Christmas, decorating their homes and giving presents. But except for the small number of Christians in Japan, it's strictly a secular observance. The Japanese calendar corresponds to ours (before the Meiji Restoration, they used the Chinese lunar calendar). But they reckon the year differently, counting from the year the current emperor began his reign. In Japan, it is now Showa 63, sixty-three years since Hirohito became emperor.

Christianity: Another Tradition

Christianity doesn't have much of a place in Japan, although I met a few people who were Christian and saw a few Christian churches. First introduced in Japan in 1549 by a Jesuit missionary, Francis Xavier, Christianity caught on quickly; soon there were about a half million converts. However, the shōgun felt their power threatened by Christianity and successfully stamped it out, murdering thousands of Christians. By the end of the nineteenth century Christianity was no longer prohibited, but this time it spread much more slowly. Today less than 1 percent of the population is Christian—about half Protestant, half Catholic.

The Christians I met happened to be Quakers, because my original contacts in Japan came through a Quaker-affiliated college. One woman told me she had become Quaker after several years of study and thought; a scholarly woman, her decision seemed to be mostly rational. For another woman, the decision was primarily emotional. She was a member of the Society of Friends, as the Quakers are called, but had previously been Roman Catholic, and before that, Protestant. Her grandfather had been a minister, although she couldn't remember what denomination. She thought it odd that I would ask the question.

"In America," she said, "Protestants disagree with Catholics, and if you're Protestant then the Baptists disagree with the Methodists and the sects all disagree with each other. In Japan, everything is mixed together, Shinto and Buddhist and Christian, and everyone gets along fine."

This is the ideal solution, she thinks; there is no reason to have strife among groups. Shinto is for marriage and the birth of a baby, Buddhism is for the funeral, and nobody sees any conflict between the two. For herself, she explained, "Jesus was knocking on the door for many years, and for many years I refused to open the door. Now I have opened it."

"And your husband?"

"He's a complete skeptic. He doesn't believe anything."

Weddings: Ceremonial Big Business

The most elaborate—and expensive—of the religious celebrations are weddings. Several years ago *Time* ran an article about Japanese weddings, noting that the average couple spends about $22,000 on their wedding, reflecting "the young generation's rebellion against reserve and modesty." About three-quarters of a million weddings take place every year, most of them in November, most of them in ceremonial halls—Tokyo has about three hundred. I saw a hall in Utsunomiya, a kind of English Tudor castle with leaded windows, stained glass, and plaster cherubs tooting trumpets from fake turrets. Generally wedding ceremonies are Shinto, although many young couples like the idea of being married in a Western church.

One day, riding on the subway with Maiko, I noticed advertisements for weddings. The ad offered A, B, and C types, the cheapest about $100 per guest, the most expensive about $120. The head charge covered "everything," including an elaborate dinner and a gift for each guest.

The bride in the advertisement wore a Western-style white gown and veil, although some brides dress in kimonos and large headdresses to hide the "horns of jealousy" Japanese tradition ascribes to women. At some weddings the bride may change her costume several times; the polite explanation is that it shows off the different facets of her personality, but the more candid is that it's to show off her family's wealth. The groom's prescribed outfit is formal and Western, including a black morning coat with a wing collar.

Hotels make a strong pitch for wedding business, competing with the ceremonial halls. International House, which offers basic accommodations to researchers and scholars visiting Tokyo from all over the world, is set on two precious acres of well-maintained grounds in the middle of the crowded city. It's favored by the Japanese intelligentsia when their children decide to marry; it has prestige and it's not as expensive as some of the ceremonial halls. My modest hotel in Utsunomiya had an entire lobby dedicated to the wedding business: a counter with several clerks on duty and one wall completely filled with shelves of gift items. In Japan, guests give money to the bride and groom, but in return receive gifts like clocks, coffee sets, tea sets, and small appliances. A couple of huge glass cases of plastic food displayed the menus available; the contents of each case represented a complete meal for ten people, including a carp and all kinds of side dishes. Prices per person ranged from about $50 to $70. Since most weddings include at least a hundred guests, the cost of food alone could easily run to $7,000.

People like to talk about the outrageous cost of weddings. Some justify the expense as a last fling before drudgery sets in: housekeeping and child-rearing for the wife, a nose-to-the-grindstone job for the husband. After the wedding the newlyweds may take off for a honeymoon in Hawaii, probably the last long trip they will have together for many years.

The Tea Ceremony: A Social Sacrament

The tea ceremony of Japan was introduced by Buddhists from China in the fifteenth century as a semireligious social custom. Japan continued the cultural evolution. Tea was originally made from a cake, which was boiled; in its next form, powdered tea was whipped—the way it's made in the tea ceremony; now in its third form, tea leaves are steeped, the way Westerners drink it. For the Chinese the tea ceremony was simply a nice way of preparing and drinking a beverage, but the Japanese developed it into an art. Some call it a "social sacrament," but it's not considered a religious rite.

Mr. Shirota brought me *The Book of Tea*, a history and philosophy of tea written in the early 1900s. He has studied the tea ceremony, and he had arranged for me to observe one of the classes with his tea master, a woman. (Traditionally tea masters have been male, but this is changing; women have the leisure to pursue the ancient art form, and women have become the teachers.) Her "tea house" was in an apartment building in an ordinary-looking neighborhood. One of her students, a girl in her twenties, opened the door for us when we rang. We took off our shoes and stepped back in time.

We entered the mat room, where a scroll and a vase with a single flower were the only decoration. The tea master was dressed in a kimono, kneeling motionless and directing activities in a gentle voice. She was probably in her forties, although her face was so serene and unlined that it was impossible to be sure. The girls took turns preparing tea and serving it to one another and to the guests. Each student had a kit, a small bag containing various personal implements used in the ceremony like the silk napkin.

In the ceremony each movement has a meaning and must be performed precisely. Kneeling in the kitchen outside the tearoom, one of the students opened the sliding door exactly halfway with her right hand, while the left hand rested on her thigh. Then she completed opening the door with her left hand, the right now resting on her thigh. Once inside, she turned and closed the door exactly halfway with one hand, the rest of the way with the other. Each movement was slow and studied. It took a long time. But time seemed to hang suspended.

The girl rose gracefully to her feet and glided across the mat, setting down her toes first, like a dancer. She knelt again in front of the small fire where water boiled in a kettle. She picked up a bamboo dipper and slowly transferred water from a large china bowl into the kettle. When she finished, she replaced the dipper precisely in a holder, her fingers at exactly the proper spot on the handle of the dipper. Removing a bright orange silk napkin from her belt, she turned it slowly, edge for edge, finally allowing it to fall into a triangle, which she then folded into a series of pleats, and began the ritual wiping of each item used for the ceremony. The container of powdered tea was removed from a silk carrying bag, the bag laid down in a certain way, the tea measured into the tea bowl.

All this time the tea master murmured encouragement, "*So so so*," and made occasional corrections in a gentle voice. Eventually the powdered green tea was placed in the tea bowl, hot water poured in, and the mixture whipped with a split-bamboo whisk.

When we had first arrived we had been served a thin slice

of sweet bean paste—to "veil the stomach," Mr. Shirota explained—before drinking the tea. I had been sitting back against the wall (Mr. Shirota had asked me to wear slacks, since he had learned that I couldn't kneel or even sit properly), watching all of this. But suddenly the student who had whipped the tea was kneeling in front of me, presenting the bowl. I didn't have the faintest idea what to do, but I managed to scramble to my knees. The student set the bowl in front of me and bowed, palms flat on the floor, forehead touching the mat. I tried to do the same. She handed me the bowl. The tea looked like algae, thick and green. With coaching from Maiko and Mr. Shirota, I rotated the bowl two turns, drank the tea down without stopping (it wasn't awful, but it wasn't great, either), rotated the bowl two turns back again, and set it down on the mat. Then I crept back to my position against the wall.

Other students took their turns with Maiko and Mr. Shirota. Two young men arrived. They started a second charcoal fire, and a second group began practicing there. They were not as far along in their training and seemed less sure of themselves. The tea master rose and glided over to encourage them, all the while making polite speeches to me, which Maiko translated. I asked if there were differences in the training of men and women. The tea master responded that men are to have more "masculine movements." I was not able to detect any differences, because they walked in the same toe-first gliding motion, knelt and opened and closed doors in the same precise, painstaking way. But then I noticed that the men's silk napkins were purple rather than brilliant orange, and they seemed to fold them over their waistbands in a somewhat different way. No one knew why the color of the napkin was different.

When it was time to leave, we went through the farewell ritual, exchanging *meishi* (hers was printed on handmade paper with ragged edges), bowing and wishing each other good fortune, and bowing again. Moments later we were out on the street. The sun had set, all the lights were blazing, the streets were noisy; we had returned suddenly and harshly to the twentieth century. Outside a restaurant a group of young men in white shirts and neckties were tossing someone up into the air and catching him with exuberant cheers apparently celebrating his promotion in his company. Back in my part of town, at Roppongi Crossing, hundreds of young people were gathered in front of the Almond, a coffee shop that had become a famous rendezvous spot, with girls on one side and boys on the other, all laughing and talking and giggling and slyly watching each other. That would be the extent of a night out for most teenagers. Older dressed-up couples strolled arm in arm, on their way to restaurants and nightclubs. It was Saturday night in Tokyo.

5
Cultural Differences: Meyer-san

Masayo

Masayo's dark hair has an oddly chopped-off look—bangs stopping too high above her eyebrows, ears barely covered, too much neck exposed. "It's a school rule," her teacher explained. "We believe that long hair can be"—she struggled for the right English word—"an *omen* of student problems."

Masayo (pronounced MAH-sah-yoh) is fifteen, in her third year of junior high school in Tokyo. Much of her daily life is controlled by school rules: the way she cuts her hair, the length of her school uniform, the style of her book bag, the way she trims her nails. In March, the end of the school year in Japan, she will take an entrance examination for high school; her three years in high school will be focused on passing entrance exams for the university.

This was a Saturday, and Masayo had just come home

from school (Japanese students attend school a half day on Saturday, until one o'clock); she brought her English teacher with her.

Masayo's grandmother had met Maiko and me at the subway station. She had no trouble picking me out; there are lots of Westerners in some parts of Tokyo, but tall, blue-eyed foreigners were less common in that part of the city, far from downtown. She bowed low in greeting and led the way through a business area, across a bridge over a highway and a canal, and finally to a two-story house crowded close to its neighbors. We left our shoes at the entrance and stepped into the scuff slippers provided for guests. Then Masayo's mother, Naoko (NAH-oh-koh), took over, leading us through a small sitting room with a TV set, through a crowded kitchen, and up a flight of steep, narrow stairs, while I struggled not to lose my slippers in the process.

At the door of the second floor "guest room," a parlor for entertaining visitors, we stepped out of the slippers. It was a traditional Japanese room with straw mats on the floor, furnished with a low table surrounded by thin cushions and a "floor chair," a legless seat with a back. That was for me. In Japan, the proper posture in a formal situation is kneeling—sitting on your heels, with your back straight. When guests are invited to relax, men sit cross-legged, but women must sit with their legs tucked to one side, less painful than kneeling but still uncomfortable for me. The floor chair made it easier to sit properly, but when Naoko suggested I stretch my legs out under the table, I did.

I was there because of Naoko's brother, Mitsuo (my friend from the University of New Mexico), who had given me a list of the people in his sister's family. Naoko's husband is Nakakazu, who is in the building materials business. The husband's parents live with them. Masayo is their oldest child. Mitsuo had made a note after her name: "Studying hard (?) to pass the entrance exam for a top-ranking high school (?). I think she is an average girl who attends junior high school and is going to take the entrance exam next spring." Next on Mitsuo's list were Kei (pronounced KAY), the ten-year-old son, and Ai (pronounced EYE and meaning "love" in Japanese), the six-year-old daughter. There was an address and telephone number.

"They are looking forward to meeting you," Mitsuo said. "The only problem is that no one in the family speaks English."

First I had to find someone to call Naoko to arrange for my visit. Then I had to decide how to get to their home. I asked Maiko to telephone Mitsuo's sister, who invited us for lunch.

While Naoko raced up and down the narrow stairway with innumerable dishes for our lunch, I had plenty of time to gawk. They didn't seem to mind; they expected me to be curious and ask questions. I noticed the little alcove formed by closets with sliding doors in which dolls and other objects were displayed. They had questions for me, too, mostly about Albuquerque. Naoko handed me a stack of snapshots from Mitsuo's wedding to Noriko several years before. She wondered how her brother and sister-in-law were getting along in America. I told her about our visit to an Indian pueblo, about traditional American food I had cooked for them, and about the wonderful Japanese meal they had fixed for us.

"*Itadaki masu*," we said and picked up our *hashi*—chopsticks. Pronounced EE-tah-dah-kee mahss (the *u* is silent), the phrase means "let us be grateful," and is almost always spoken at the beginning of a meal. This was indeed a meal to be grateful for, perhaps a dozen different dishes, some of which I recognized, some I didn't. Labor-intensive, it must have kept Naoko busy in the kitchen for a couple of hours. Nakakazu stopped by to meet me, but like many Japanese men, he worked all day Saturday. The grandmother had disappeared; Kei and Ai apparently had not been invited. Guests at the table included Masayo and her English teacher, a pleasant young woman with shaky English. Maiko had the job of interpreter.

After we had eaten and were sipping little cups of green tea, Masayo showed me her bedroom, a small room crowded with a Western-style bed, a narrow wardrobe, a desk, and a spinet piano. Through Maiko she asked me, "Do you have *meishi?*" Masayo was starting a collection.

Speaking slowly, using simple vocabulary and basic sentence structure, I tried to get Masayo to talk to me. English is required of all Japanese students, and she has been studying for three years. I asked her what she was studying in English. After a whispered consultation with her English teacher, she answered: "Grammar."

"What kind of grammar?" I pushed her.

More whispers and some giggles. "Past perfect tense," she announced.

I struggled to remember exactly what that was. They saw the struggle and laughed. "You're a writer," Maiko said. "You're supposed to know what it is."

Before I left, I presented my gift to Naoko—a woolen mat handwoven in Albuquerque in the traditional style of early Spanish weavers of the area. I had, in fact, about two dozen of these mats in my suitcase. Gift giving is an important part of Japanese life, and one gift always deserves another. Masayo presented their gift to me: three fine handkerchiefs.

The grandmother was downstairs when we left. She knelt, placing the palms of her hands flat on the floor, and bowed until her forehead also touched the floor. Maiko quickly knelt and returned the bow while I stood there awkwardly, wondering what on earth I was supposed to do.

Masayo's family was the first I met in Japan. I don't know

how typical they were, but they did serve as an introduction to a society and a culture vastly different from our own.

"Not another book about slippers and chopsticks!" groaned a young Japanese when he heard I was writing a book about Japan.

"No," I said, "but that's part of it."

Japan is changing. This doesn't mean it is becoming Westernized, as many people on both sides of the Pacific sometimes think. Just because young people wear jeans and love rock music is no more a sign of Americanization than our craze for Japanese food and cars means we are becoming "Japanized." I wanted to learn what I could about the society and how the changes affected young Japanese. It was a lot to take on.

I was deeply conscious of my Americanness. Language was a big part of it, but even when I was with people who spoke English fluently, I was always uncomfortably aware that I wasn't sure what "good manners" meant to the Japanese. In America, when you meet someone, you look them in the eye (good eye contact), speak up clearly (no self-effacing mumbles), and shake hands firmly (no fishy grip). But that is considered aggressive behavior in Japan, definitely not the way a Japanese woman greets a man. As it turned out, I had less trouble with the public encounters— introductions to school officials, for instance—when I simply tried to do what everyone else did, than with the private ones, when I was a guest and a stranger in someone's home. Often in Japan the voice I heard most was inside my own head, asking "What do I do now?"

The Japanese Home

In the past, the traditional Japanese home was a small wooden house with sliding doors and partitions, called *shoji*, made of translucent paper. Compressed straw mats, called *tatami*, covered the floor. In the center of the room was an opening with a table over it; in winter the family sat around the table with a heavy quilt thrown over it, and a charcoal brazier in the opening warmed their feet and legs. A closet with sliding doors covered part of one wall; bedding was stored in the closet, and the space at the end of the closet formed an alcove, *tokonoma*, where family treasures were displayed. At night, thick cotton pads—futons—were pulled out of the closet, laid out on the floor, and covered with quilts. The family slept together.

Today most of the old wooden houses with thatched roofs have disappeared, except for some out in the country. Most people live in cramped apartments in concrete block buildings. Many have at least one "mat room" with *tatami* on the floor, but the mats are more expensive than carpet and few can afford to have them in every room. The mats measure 90 by 180 centimeters, and room sizes are described by the number of mats it takes to cover the floor: a "4½-mat room" is quite small; a "6-mat room" is average. The edges of expensive mats are bound in brocade; cheaper ones, in cotton. It's bad manners to step on the seams. Modern Japanese carpet the floors that don't have mats, but some mix the two styles, putting a square of carpeting in the center of the room under the low table. Halls and stairs are of natural wood; stairs are steep and narrow, to conserve space.

Although some Japanese have adopted Western-style beds, most still prefer to pull out futons at night and sleep on the floor, covered with down-filled quilts. The Japanese might serve formal meals at the low table in the mat room, but there is probably a Western-style table and chairs in the kitchen, if there's room, or dining area. Some use floor chairs, which provide a backrest (and even armrests) for sitting on the floor. Electric heaters have replaced charcoal braziers under the table, but there is still no central heating.

The style of the Japanese home affects the way people behave there, and when I was a guest, I struggled to figure out what was expected of me. In one home the mother and children made up my bed for me, laying the futon on the floor with a couple of quilts and a large towel. I didn't know what the towel was for, or which layers I was to sleep between. The son demonstrated by crawling beneath the towel. Later, I learned that towels are used instead of sheets in the summer. Since the Japanese do not customarily travel with pajamas or nightgowns, they left me a *yukata*, a kimono-like cotton robe with a long sash. (Hotels provide their guests with *yukata*.) But I didn't know exactly how to wear it—left side over right, or the other way around? I had read somewhere that one is correct and the other means something unpleasant, but I couldn't remember which was which. I didn't know how to tie the sash. I didn't know whether it was all right to be seen wearing this robe around the house, or if that was some breach of etiquette. (As it turned out, *yukata* are worn in place of kimonos in summer and on informal occasions. I could have gone out on the street in it.)

Then there was the problem of the pillow. It was hard, like a sack of rice, and it crunched like a sack of rice. I got rid of it and wadded up one of the quilts under my head. Not that I needed any blankets at all: it was very hot in Japan, and my hosts had pulled down the metal shutters outside my windows and locked them. My room was like an oven, and I couldn't figure out how to sneak open a window, so I could breathe.

The next morning the family asked if I had slept well. I lied and said I had. I didn't ask about the locked shutters, but I did ask about the crunchy pillow. The son consulted his English dictionary. "Buckwheat," he said. His older brother explained: "Buckwheat is good for you to sleep on, especially in summer. It keeps the brain cool." But buckwheat is expensive, I found out, and only the best pillows are filled with them. Cheaper pillows are mostly synthetic with only a little buckwheat stitched into a pocket on one side. The next night I had a less exotic pillow. I slept much better, although the shutters were again closed.

One of the first techniques I had to master in Japan was the use of slippers. The Japanese *never* wear street shoes inside the house; most schools and many public buildings also require everyone to leave their shoes at the entrance. Between the front door at ground level and the step up to the living area is a small space for exchanging shoes for slippers; most hosts keep several pairs for visitors. When you step out of your shoes, you don't do it just any which way but manage it so that your shoes never touch the top of the step and your feet don't touch ground level; you must also set both shoes facing the door, so that when you are ready to leave, you can step back into them gracefully. In some places a long-handled shoehorn hangs nearby so that you don't have to bend over. Most adults wear shoes that slip on and off easily; lace-up shoes are hard to manage. But most students wear sneakers, and the backs are usually broken down from sliding in and out of them without un-doing the laces maybe a dozen times a day.

Once inside the house, you must remember to step out of the slippers before you go into a room with *tatami*. And you *never* wear them into the toilet room, where a pair of wooden clogs or special toilet slippers waits inside. It's a major breach of etiquette to wear house slippers into the toilet room, but even worse to forget to change when you come out and to walk through the house in toilet slippers— comparable in our culture to appearing in public in your underwear (not quite indecent, but simply not done). Only once did I commit this unpardonable social gaffe; fortunately, no one saw me.

The toilet room in a Japanese house is always separate from the bathroom, which is strictly for bathing. The homes I visited had Western-style commodes installed in tiny cubicles, some of them equipped with electrically warmed seats, a nicety in winter since the cubicles are not heated. Public toilets are quite different. Most department stores, restaurants, schools, and office buildings have the traditional Japanese squat toilet, an oval porcelain bowl sunk in the floor. In some, you're expected to leave your shoes in the hall and wear clogs into the toilet room. There are advocates for both types of toilet, each side claiming superior sanitary and physiological advantages. Fortunately one of my tourist brochures included a photograph with a slipper placed on each side of the bowl, illustrating how to deal with this unfamiliar contraption.

Since most upper-class Japanese now have hot water in their houses and bathe at home, I didn't get a chance to experience a public bath. The typical Japanese bathroom is like a large shower stall with a short, deep tub. There is a flexible shower hose outside the tub and a drain in the floor. The idea is to scrub yourself thoroughly outside the tub, shower off, and then soak in the tub brimming with hot water. The point of the bath is not to clean yourself—you've already done that—but to relax. You save the water for the next family member, in order of seniority (Honored Guests go first), and the tub can be covered to keep the water hot.

On my first overnight visit with a Japanese family, I was

offered a bath. They had entertained me with a lavish dinner, and we were lingering over coffee at the end of the meal. One of the sons left the table, came back a few minutes later and said, "Please take bath."

I didn't want a bath then; I prefer a quick shower in the morning. I was enjoying the company at the table, and I really didn't want a hot bath after the big meal. But in Japan, you don't say no. So I went to take a bath.

Then the problems began. Was I supposed to wear my slippers into the little dressing room outside the bathroom? Just in case, I left them outside. Then I couldn't figure out which was the soap. There was no soap bar, only several plastic bottles of liquid, the labels all in Japanese. Which was for showering? I picked something green. When I thought I had scrubbed and rinsed enough, I climbed into the tub, thinking of boiled lobsters and steamed clams. How long was I supposed to sit there? In the next room—the bathroom is usually next to the kitchen—I could hear sounds of cleaning up. I guessed that I had been sent to take a bath to get me out of the way; they would not wash the dishes in the presence of the Honored Guest, and would never dream of letting me help. So I stayed submerged until the clattering stopped.

Next dilemma: should I put on my street clothes or the cotton sleeping robe? It was after nine o'clock, and I wanted some time to collect my thoughts and make a few notes. But maybe that would be considered rude: maybe they expected me to chat with them for a while. Afraid to risk the *yukata* in public, I got dressed again, combed my wet hair, and went into the large mat room, where the family was watching television. Immediately they produced green tea and a plate of sliced pears. We struggled with conversation. How long was I expected to stay? When was bedtime? When I thought enough time had passed, I said good night and went to my room. Moments later, all the lights went out and the house grew silent. I wondered how long they had been waiting for the American to quit talking and go to bed.

Japanese Food

The Japanese diet is good for you; some say it's the best in the world. It uses very little fat. Most of the protein comes from fish or soybean products, occasionally from chicken, but almost never from beef, which is incredibly expensive. Rice is the staple, although it's polished and has therefore lost a good source of fiber. Traditionally the Japanese eat rice at all three meals, although that's changing: they now eat bread at one or two meals. There are few fat people, except for the legendary *sumo* wrestlers; obesity has never been a problem, but that's changing, too. Fast foods have come to Japan from the United States, and Japanese kids gobble up Big Macs and the Colonel's fried chicken. The change in diet shows: more kids are overweight, and parents and teachers worry about the children's eating habits.

Japanese cuisine is world-class, beautiful in the way it's served, a delicate blend of subtle flavors. But usually unless it's for a special event, the food in ordinary restaurants is several cuts below "cuisine": lots of plain boiled rice, lots of noodles, little bits of fish processed in unfamiliar ways, unidentifiable vegetables. Except when I was invited to someone's home for dinner, or when friends took me out, I ate in inexpensive restaurants, and the food got boring.

Since I couldn't read the menu, I took advantage of the wonderful Japanese custom of displaying, in cases outside the restaurant, highly realistic plastic models of the dishes available. I would study these models, trying to figure out what was in them, and when I found something that looked appetizing and was within my budget, I would go inside and gesture for someone to come out and see what it was I wanted. (The "follow me" gesture is done fingers *down*; fingers up, as we do it, is insulting.) But what I was served was often still a surprise and usually didn't look as good as the plastic model—the shrimp weren't nearly as big, and there weren't as many of them.

Raw fish in *sushi* and *sashimi* is an expensive delicacy. In *tempura* restaurants, fish and vegetables are dipped in batter and deep-fried, and *yakitori* restaurants serve chicken grilled on skewers. *Okonomi-yaki*, advertised in tourist areas as "Japanese pizza," is cooked on a grill built into the table; you mix stiff batter and a raw egg with all kinds of chopped vegetables, fish, or meat and spice it up with flaked fish and seaweed while it fries like a big pancake. Perhaps the most unusual restaurant was a country place near a waterfall where noodles flowed through a bamboo trough; the trick was to grab them with chopsticks as they whooshed by (the noodles were collected in a colander at the end of the trough, for people like me who weren't good noodle catchers).

I tried everything I was offered and usually liked it, with the exception of *natto*, fermented soybeans that are gummy and taste like something gone bad. Traditionally *natto* is mixed with rice for breakfast. I did eat Japanese breakfast a few times—rice (without *natto*), a bowl of *miso*, some fish and vegetables—but generally I took the option of an American breakfast of eggs and toast.

I got used to eating with *hashi*, chopsticks, although at first I held them in such a fierce grip that my hand got tired before the end of the meal. A bowl of plain boiled rice is usually placed on the left and a lacquer bowl of *miso*, on the right. You drink the *miso* from the bowl, holding it with four fingers supporting the base and your thumb on the rim. You hold the rice bowl the same way, near the middle of your chest, instead of trying to get the rice into your mouth from table level. Noodles come in many forms, and noodle shops are everywhere, filled at lunchtime with office workers slurping loudly and quickly. Noodle slurping is considered good manners in Japan; so is eating fast.

The Japanese are fond of fruit as a dessert or a snack, but there's a right and a wrong way to eat it. Large purple grapes are served on the stem. I popped the grapes into my mouth, discovered that the skins were thick and tough, and not easy to swallow; and spit the skin out with the seeds into the palm of my hand. Wrong move: the Japanese daintily peel each grape. Japanese pears are sweet and juicy, round and yellow like large apples. They are pared and sliced and served impaled on tiny forks; you nibble around the fork down to the last bite.

Japanese Customs

"Do you think the Japanese are formal?" a student asked.

"Compared to Americans, very formal," I said.

The Japanese see the relaxed informality of Americans as somewhat barbaric. There is our habit of using first names, which the Japanese call "personal names," to differentiate them from "family names." (Traditionally in Japan the family name is written before the personal name.) Although I stayed in people's homes, spent time with them, and got to know them at least a little, no one ever called me Carolyn. (It's a difficult name for Japanese to pronounce, with the *r* and the *l*. My Japanese friends in Albuquerque have adopted the first-name habit, but they usually mispronounce it: it comes out "Caloryn" or sometimes "Caroryn.") In Japan I was always "Meyer-san." *San* is the polite form of address that means "Mr.," "Mrs.," and "Miss." English-speaking Japanese called me Mrs. Meyer. And sometimes I heard myself being referred to as *sensei* (SEHN-say), a respectful term meaning "teacher."

On the other hand, I never called anyone except young students by their personal names. Mrs. Murata, who is exactly my age, with whom I spent hours each day for several days, and who discussed all sorts of intimate matters with me, always called me Mrs. Meyer. I thought of suggesting that she call me Carolyn, but I preferred to see if she would take the initiative and ask me to call her by her personal name. She never did, and I always called her Mrs. Murata.

And we always bowed when we met. Everyone bows to everyone else, arms at the sides. Sometimes it's not much more than a bob of the head; sometimes it's a deep bow from the waist. Girls who come through the high-speed bullet trains selling food and drinks invariably face the passengers and bow to no one in particular before dragging the food cart through to the next car. Young women in white gloves greet customers at the entrances of huge department stores with a bow.

I had read that mothers begin to train their children to bow while they are still babies, pushing down the child's head whenever they meet someone. That's not done so much anymore, a young mother told me, but children must still learn how to express respect in bowing: the higher the other person is in the social structure, the lower one must bow. Children and teachers bow to one another at the beginning and end of classes. Although some Japanese have adopted the Western custom of shaking hands, I bowed unless someone offered a hand to shake. As a foreigner, I was not expected to understand the slight differences in seniority, but I did my best to conform, bowing lower to a high school principal, for instance, than to the English teacher. You bow when you meet someone, and you bow when you leave—sometimes several times.

The Japanese are controlled in their body movements;

their gestures are economical, perhaps because they live in such confined spaces. I had to concentrate on keeping my gestures small and my voice quiet. At a formal occasion like a dinner or a tea ceremony, the proper posture is to kneel, sitting back on your heels. Most adults who have been brought up since early childhood to maintain this position for long periods of time seem perfectly comfortable, but after only a couple of minutes my legs began to cramp; more than a few minutes became real torture. Young people who haven't been trained to kneel formally looked just as miserable as I. Since Japanese hosts don't want their foreign guests to suffer, they always invited me to sit however I liked.

The Japanese have a reputation for being unfailingly polite. Their behavior toward me surpassed mere politeness: they were remarkably kind, often going far out of their way to help.

One rainy morning in a trolley in Hiroshima, I missed the street where my hotel was located. An elderly man, guessing I was lost, spoke to the motorman, who stopped the trolley. I showed them the paper with the name of the hotel written in Japanese. The old man got off the trolley and motioned me to follow. He picked up my bag and walked at a fast clip about six blocks to the hotel with me stumbling after him. He spoke no English. He carried my bag into the lobby, bowed, smiled, and left.

People on trains and subways often helped me find what I was looking for. When I couldn't figure out which subway exit to take to reach the Kabukiza Theater in Tokyo, two women, one in her sixties, led me up a long flight of stairs to the theater entrance. A young man on a subway who overheard me asking another foreigner how to get to a certain department store took me there himself. A well-dressed woman I met on a train guided me through the underground maze to the subway I was supposed to take. And this wasn't just "small-town friendliness"—this was in one of the largest cities in the world.

How the Japanese Relax

When it comes to relaxation, in some ways Japanese are not much different from Americans: everybody is hooked on television, and teachers complain that students spend too much time playing video games. Teenagers listen to rock music. Everybody loves baseball, and businessmen play a lot of golf.

But some kinds of entertainment are uniquely Japanese. One Sunday I went to the Kabukiza Theater to see *Gompachi's Nightmare*, one part of a four-part program and the most I wanted to sit through not understanding the language or the art form. (*Kabuki* developed in the sixteenth and seventeenth centuries, becoming more popular than the classical *Noh* drama that preceded it.) According to the program, "A young warrior, Gompachi, is arrested for his crimes and sentenced to death. Tied and bound, he is led on horseback to the place of execution when his lover, the courtesan Komurasaki, comes to his rescue and cuts his ropes. At least that is what seems to be happening."

The theater was crowded; up in the cheap balcony seats where I sat, young kids, elderly women in kimonos, and a handful of tourists drank green tea and ate *bento*, Japanese box lunches, waiting for the play to begin. Drums signaled the entrance of the characters from the back of the theater. The first scene was set in the country, where the courtesan did seem to be rescuing the hero from execution. But the second scene changed suddenly to a court with cherry blossoms and festival lanterns. When the curtain came down after thirty-five minutes, I had no idea what had happened. The costumes and stage set were magnificent, the stylized acting was interesting (female impersonators play the roles of women), and the music performed by two lute players and four singers in an unfamiliar tonality, probably an acquired taste. Several rows in front of me, a man who apparently knew the play well shouted occasionally to the actors. My program described this practice as "a form of applause demanding good timing and artistic sense."

To tell the truth, I enjoyed the singing in the *karaoke* bars much more. Japanese men customarily stop off at a bar to drink on their way home from work. In the old days they were entertained by *geisha*, women trained to sing, play the lute, serve *sake* (rice wine), and amuse their customers with witty conversation. The elegant geisha in kimonos have been replaced by bar girls who serve drinks and chat with their customers. But sometimes the customers entertain each other, in *karaoke* bars equipped with electronic sound equipment that provides musical accompaniment and enhances the vocal quality of the singer. The soloist grabs the microphone and, prompted by lyrics flashed on a small screen in front of him, belts out or croons his favorite song, while on the big screen behind him a video sets the mood.

One night several Japanese schoolteachers took me out for a night on the town in Utsunomiya. The last stop was a *karaoke* bar, where my friends took their turns at the mike. Then it was my turn. I didn't need much coaxing. From the small list of songs in English I picked "Tennessee Waltz" and pretended to be Patti Page, while fences, horses, cows, and a shot of the Tennessee state line unrolled behind me.

Later I described the adventure to an American schoolteacher. "You're lucky," she said. "I tried it one night and discovered halfway through 'You Are My Sunshine' that the video was a porn film."

Always easy to spot, *pachinko* parlors are everywhere, in the middle of town or out on the highway—the places with the most garish neon on the outside, the brightest lights on the inside. Pachinko has been described as "vertical pinball." Players buy a box of stainless-steel balls, which they pour into a trough that feeds the machine. At the rate of about one per second, the balls are released and shot up a metal track; the player fiddles with a knob to control how high the little ball will go. Then it begins to drop, ricocheting off metal pins and plastic flippers. If you're lucky, the ball is deflected into a cup that wins you points and ultimately more balls. If you're like me, the ball drops out of sight with no score, and in less time than it takes me to write about it, several dollars' worth of balls have simply disappeared.

I went on a Saturday morning with Steve, an American friend, who apparently clocks a lot of time in pachinko parlors. The place was jammed and noisy. Middle-aged couples played on adjacent machines, a little girl patiently watched her mother, young men and old men stared hypnotized at the flying balls. A hundred or so machines make a lot of racket as the balls race through, tootling electronic tunes as the scores run up. I lost all my balls in no time, but Steve managed to keep his going, losing some but collecting payoffs often enough. You can either keep playing until you lose all the balls or, if you're good, cash in the ones you win. Steve got bored eventually with the machine he had been playing, although he was winning fairly consistently, and moved on to a row of machines with a higher risk factor: it was harder to score, but the payoff was bigger.

Sometimes he wins a few thousand yen, Steve says, and sometimes he loses. That day he was losing. Convinced that the machines were rigged, he was also convinced that all the machines would eventually pay off, and he was determined to stick with one he felt had to open up at any moment—maybe on the very next play. It didn't happen. He went through all his yen before we left.

Pachinko and *karaoke* are illegal for teenagers, but music is not. "MICHAEL JACKSON FEVER EXPECTED TO BE BIGGER THAN MADONNA FEVER" proclaimed the headline, and for the next couple of weeks the American star was major news. When Madonna hit Japan earlier in the year, $45 tickets were scalped for $350; police watched for similar exploits with Jackson's eleven appearances in Japan. No sooner had Jackson fever subsided than Jon Bon Jovi made the scene. Teenagers turned out in droves, greeting the American rock group with what the press described as "a rare display of Japanese enthusiasm." Most of the audience was conservatively dressed, some in school uniforms, a few mavericks in long hair and leather. Two optimistic schoolgirls showed up in white wedding gowns.

6
Cultural Differences:
Gaijin

Katherine

Katherine knows all about loneliness. A half-dozen years ago she was an insider like Gina, living with a family. An exchange student from South Dakota, she spent a year in Utsunomiya. She loved the experience and made up her mind to come back to Japan to live and work. Now she's just another *gaijin*.

Gaijin, the Japanese word for foreigner, literally means "outsider," and applies to everyone not of Japanese ancestry, to anyone not born and raised in Japan. The Japanese have a reputation for being extremely xenophobic (*xenos* is the Greek word for "stranger"; *xenophobic* means fearful or contemptuous of strangers or foreigners). I sometimes wondered what would happen if I decided to stay in Japan and give up my special status as Honored Guest. Like Katherine and other *gaijin*, I'd have to endure some fairly massive

81

culture shock until I found where I fit—or didn't fit—into Japanese society.

Katherine, a vivacious woman with a dazzling smile, had graduated from college two years before and was chosen to come to Japan as part of the Japanese Exchange and Teaching Program run by the Japanese Ministry of Education. English-speaking teaching assistants work in teams with Japanese teachers. Out of 4,495 applicants from the U.S., United Kingdom, Australia, and New Zealand, 817 were accepted. Katherine was one of them.

Assigned to a prefectural suboffice in a small town in Tochigi-ken, Katherine spends one day a week in the office shuffling papers, the other days circulating among the schools. The previous year she had forty-four schools on her roster; at each school she made a "self-introduction," talking about herself in English. That was the extent of her contact.

"I got very burned out doing that," Katherine admits. "You can't do a thing with forty-four schools. This year I've got only seventeen. I'm getting better at working with the English teachers in the school. I tell them 'No choral reading.' That's how they've been teaching conversation—everybody reads aloud together. The kids don't learn anything."

But the burnout isn't the only problem: Katherine is having a difficult time in other ways. Once an insider, she is now an outsider. The people in her office are much older and they go their separate ways at the end of the day. Katherine goes home to her tiny apartment with two rooms—one 8' × 10', the other 6' × 8', plus a minuscule kitchen—for which she pays about three hundred dollars a month in rent. There is no heat, no hot water. A small kerosene heater keeps the pipes from freezing, but she worries about suffocating. The winters in this part of Japan are severe; everyone dresses in layer upon layer of clothing.

"Last year I went home to South Dakota at Christmas to warm up," she said.

The night before we met, there was a fire in a shop two doors from her apartment. In the middle of the night someone had awakened her and told her to leave. When she opened the door, she saw a wall of flame. Frightened, she grabbed her wallet and her mother's diamond earrings and fled. "I thought to myself, this is what loneliness is all about."

We discussed some of the cultural differences that make it hard for Americans to adjust to living in Japan: eye contact is restrained, and it's better to speak hesitantly, to show humility—the exact opposite of what Americans are taught. We are also taught to express our feelings and to say what we think. In Japan such openness is actively discouraged—it indicates too much individuality. "Tell me how you feel," a friend sometimes urges me. "After all, I'm not a mind reader." But the Japanese *are* mind readers, or at least expert at intuiting what other Japanese are thinking. They pay close attention to others—not just to what is said but to all that is *not* said.

For Katherine, going home last winter made things even worse; she was depressed when she came back, and it took her several months to work her way out of it. Recently things have been getting better. She joined an international group and has met some people and made a few friends, some of them other foreigners, some Japanese.

"Are you going to stay?"

"I don't know," she said.

A few weeks after I left Japan, I got a note from her. "I'm going to Nikko over the holidays," she wrote. "I have decided to stay in Japan for another year."

Steve

Bored with his life in the United States and looking for a change, Steve went to Japan a few years ago with a girl-friend; they broke up soon after they arrived, and a couple of months later he met Masako. Eventually they began to date. American men are often considered good catches by Japanese women, who perceive them as less chauvinistic and more interested in an equal relationship than Japanese males. Masako was also looking for a change; she wanted to go to the United States to improve her English.

I met Masako soon after she had arrived in Albuquerque to study English at the university. At the end of the semester she told me she was going home. I took her out for a farewell lunch, and that's when I heard about Steve. He had stayed in Japan, and she was anxious to see him again. "I didn't realize how much I would miss him," she said. "I think we will live together. But I hate to tell my parents. They will not approve."

Masako is thirty-two years old and has never been married. "Over the hill," one of my friends commented, and I heard it in somewhat less crude terms from Japanese. At thirty-two, her prospects for marriage are dim and getting dimmer.

A few months later she wrote to me, sending her new address. She had gotten an office job, she reported without enthusiasm, and she was very happy with Steve. "He helps with the laundry," she wrote. "No Japanese men do that!" She invited me to visit them in Miyazaki, in the southern part of Kyushu.

Masako picked me up at the train station. "We're getting married in December," she told me in the taxi.

They've rented a house, large by Japanese standards, with a mat room, kitchen, toilet room, and bathroom on the first floor; a smaller mat room and tiny television room (with a Western-style armchair) upstairs. The washing machine stands outside the front door, typically about half the size of an American washer, designed to fit the tight quarters of a Japanese house.

Steve was teaching an English conversation class that night; his visa permits him to work only twenty hours a week, and like most foreigners, he uses those hours to teach English. The rest of the time he studies Japanese language and culture—conversation, *kanji* (calligraphy), and *ikebana* (the art of flower arranging). And he does the laundry.

The next morning, Saturday, Steve fixed omelets for breakfast. Then Masako rode off to work on her motor scooter; while we waited for her to come back so we could all go sightseeing, Steve and I went for a walk along the river.

"How do you get along with Masako's parents?" I asked.

"I don't," he said. "We're planning to get married, but they're totally against it."

"Why?"

"Because I'm *gaijin*. There are plenty of reasons for them to object: I'm fourteen years older than Masako, I'm divorced, I've got two kids back home. I don't have a real job. But it's the fact that I'm a foreigner that really drives them crazy. For a long time they wouldn't invite me to their house. Then they came by to visit Masako, to see how she's living. Our house is as good as theirs, maybe better, so that was all right. But they've told her we can't invite any of their friends or relatives to the wedding. She's pretty upset."

(Not all Japanese parents react this way. Gina had told me about another exchange student, David, who had fallen in love with a Japanese girl. "*His* host parents won't allow him to go out to meet her, but *her* parents seem not to object too much, probably because marrying an American husband is an okay thing.")

"Maybe you'd better just elope to Hawaii," I suggested to Steve.

"Of course we can get married anywhere. But it's important to Masako to have a wedding. And her parents have to face the fact that at thirty-two, it's fairly unlikely she's going to find a Japanese to marry her."

When I saw them, Steve seemed quite at home in Japan; if he had gone through any culture shock, it was either behind him or it didn't show. Steve likes the slow pace of Miyazaki, a small city as far from Tokyo as you can get. He enjoys the culture. The whole setup suits him fine.

Masako was the one who talked about leaving. She was anxious to get away from the city where she had grown up and where job opportunities were so limited. Masako wanted to go back to America.

Around New Year's I got a card from them with a photograph of them both in kimonos, wedding finery. "We got married on December 5," Masako wrote. "As my parents got upset with me about my wedding, we had a small party. But we enjoyed the party and are living together very happily." She said she was thinking about getting another job.

Louise

It's a tiny hole-in-the-wall with a string of red lanterns outside signifying that it's a place to drink beer. Inside is a bar with six or eight stools and two small tables. Behind the bar a woman with glossy black hair tucked behind her ears cooks a variety of snacks and passes them over to the customers; most of the customers are drinking beer or *shochu*, a clear liquor something like vodka. In the corner a rather tall Japanese man with a mustache and a white T-shirt talks with customers. He keeps one eye on the television—baseball again, the national obsession. His American nickname is Ken.

Louise spends almost every evening here; she says it's her second home. Louise came to Japan several years ago to study the primary schools. Her life in the United States was falling apart then: she had broken up with a lover, her father had died, and she had flunked the orals for her doctorate. She pulled herself together and passed the exams on the second try, got a grant, and left for Japan to begin her research. But things have not gone as she planned. She got a job teaching in a junior high school and lost interest in the project. And she fell in love with Ken, the owner of the bar.

They're thinking of getting married, she said, swearing me to secrecy. They have a lot of things to figure out first— one being their very different life-styles. She teaches all day. He operates a bar until late at night. Even their days off don't coincide.

Louise describes Ken as a dropout who didn't get caught up in the Japanese educational rat race but who attended technical school for a while. His pub is a neighborhood gathering place for people as much interested in conversation as in drinking. The people who gather there are tradesmen and shopkeepers, not the stereotypical *sarariman* ("salaryman") who goes through sixteen years of school and spends the rest of his life working for a corporation.

I met Louise on my first day in Tokyo. She got me a subway map in English, explained how the fare system worked, and then abandoned me to find my own way back to Roppongi. It was a scary but highly effective initiation. Later she took me to Ken's to talk and drink *shochu* and eat whatever snacks the woman behind the counter had to offer.

"The typical Japanese male chauvinist thing of 'Hey you, go get me a beer' doesn't operate with Ken," Louise said. "I'd never settle for that dynamic." (The *Japan Times* reported a survey revealing that two out of ten Japanese husbands address their wives as *oi*, which translates as "hey you.") Ken is forty-five and has never been married; at thirty-six, neither has Louise. Both are very independent, she says. The one problem Louise has encountered so far is that if they're discussing something and Ken is uncomfortable with it, he simply shuts down and leaves. "And he has to be the one in charge of the relationship," she said. "When I try to direct it, he withdraws."

When I returned to Tokyo for a couple of days at the end of my trip, Louise and I got together again at Ken's bar. She said, "After all the traveling you've done in the past month and after all you've seen of mainstream Japanese males with their upward striving, surely you understand why I'm attracted to Ken and to this place." I did—yet on the other hand, I didn't. Surely, I thought, she must know what she's getting into with a cross-cultural marriage, with two totally different sets of expectations. But I was curious about how the romance had progressed during the month: there was no outward sign that any bond existed between them. Louise and I sat in the bar like any two customers and paid for our own food and drinks. Ken didn't talk to her. I didn't know if their liaison was a secret from the steady customers, as it was from Louise's school, or if this was the way a Japanese male customarily ignores his fiancée.

"We haven't seen much of each other," she said. "I've been busy with the opening of school. I've hinted that I have tomorrow off, but so far he hasn't reacted to the hint."

As she walked with me to find a cab back to my hotel, she said, "I really love Japan. I could spend the rest of my life here. It suits me fine. But Ken wants to go to America. He wants to open a restaurant there."

Patricia

Patricia was the only black I saw in Japan, but she claims there are enough dark-skinned people in Tokyo so that she goes there when she wants to "get lost." It's impossible for her to get lost in Utsunomiya, where she lives in what she describes as a "convent situation," surrounded by employees of the board of education of the prefecture where she teaches. Her neighbor John, a New Zealander, is also a teacher. But his life is much different, she says.

"John is very well cared for by the neighbors," she told me. "They cook for him and do things for him. They don't cook for me."

Not because of her color, I suspected, but because of her sex. Or, more to the point, because of *his* sex. Japanese males aren't supposed to know how to cook or take care of themselves—that's what women are for.

I asked Patricia if she had experienced any discrimination. The Japanese are known to be prejudiced against anyone who is not Japanese; they are especially rough on Koreans, who are from the same genetic stock. Even Koreans born in Japan of Japanese-born parents are treated like second-class citizens—like blacks in America.

"Exposure to white American values on television has made the Japanese prejudiced, too," she said, although she didn't say how she knew that. "But it's not as bad here as it is at home."

Hiroshima: Gaijin's *Pilgrimage*

Hiroshima was the only city I visited during my month in Japan where I knew no one, had no contacts of any sort. I suppose I preferred it that way. It was to be a pilgrimage to the scene of the devastation caused by the first atomic bomb, dropped on August 6, 1945.

Hiroshima is a big industrial city with a population approaching a million, built at a river mouth on Honshu. A few blocks from my small business hotel was a shopping arcade containing everything from Dunkin' Donuts and a Laura Ashley boutique to pachinko parlors and kimono shops. Hiroshima was a prime target during World War II because a large army base was located there; it was the communication center for that part of Japan, and it was a heavy industrial center. But it became the target for the A-bomb somewhat by chance: Niigata, a main port on the west coast of northern Honshu, was the first choice until heavy clouds moved in over the city; the weather in Hiroshima was reported as clear. Meanwhile, an all-night air-raid warning had been lifted in Hiroshima, and on the morning of August 6, life went on as usual in war-torn Japan. Children left for school, mailmen began their rounds.

Without warning, an American bomber appeared in the sky, released three parachutes (people on the ground thought the object they carried was a weather balloon), and took off at a sharp angle to the north. Seconds later, the bomb exploded in midair with the force of twenty thousand tons of TNT. More than 130,000 people were killed and 90 percent of the city was leveled.

Today the city has been completely rebuilt, like all the other Japanese cities severely damaged by firebombings. Across the street from my hotel was a primary school with a plaque, in Japanese and English, noting that the original school on the site was destroyed and all the teachers and pupils in it killed that morning, less than a half mile from the epicenter, the point directly below the exploding bomb.

Peace Memorial Park lies near the center of Hiroshima, where grass and trees and a museum attract busloads of tourists and school groups each day. At one end is the A-Bomb

Dome, once the Industrial Promotion Hall. It is the only bombed ruin in the city allowed to stand, its twisted steel skeleton looming above one of the branches of the Ota River. This was the autumnal equinox, a national holiday. Families rowed boats and couples strolled beneath the trees.

My first stop was the museum, jammed with groups of high school students. I rented a cassette that explained the exhibits and made my way past enlarged photographs of the dead and wounded and past glass cases with models of victims showing how clothing was burned off, flesh shredded. Next door, an art gallery exhibited stunning paintings of the bombing and its aftermath. Two small theaters ran videotapes, in Japanese and English, of Hiroshima and Nagasaki (bombed three days later)—horrible graphic depictions of the mutilations, accompanied by discussions of the radiation sickness that killed people who survived the initial blast.

I was deeply moved by what I saw; my feelings were in stark contrast to the holiday mood the Japanese seemed to be enjoying. Two schoolgirls approached me with a note: "Please read this! These girls are learning to speak English and we want a message of peace from you." I tried to talk to them. "We don't speak English," they chorused. I scribbled a message.

The statue of a girl holding aloft a crane, the symbol of peace, was half buried beneath strings of *origami* paper cranes. There must have been hundreds of strings, and hundreds of cranes in each string—some all in white, some in bright colors, some tiny, some large, heaped several feet deep. A group of schoolchildren gathered around the statue, preparing to add their cranes to the thousands already there.

Not far from the statue stands the cenotaph, a monument erected in honor of those killed by the bomb. Under the huge vault a stone chest contains a roll of those killed and bears this epitaph in Japanese: *Repose ye in peace, for the error shall not be repeated.*

Part Two

JAPANESE SCHOOLS: TRAINING FOR THE GROUP

7

The Right Start

Three Little Pigs and the Creative Spark

"Little pig, little pig, let me come in!"
"Not by the hair of my chinny-chin-chin!"
"Then I'll huff and I'll puff and I'll
  blow your house down!"

In the American version of this tale, the wolf huffs and puffs and blows down the flimsy houses of the first two little pigs, then gobbles them up. But the third little pig, safe in his sturdy brick house, lures the wolf down the chimney to his doom in a pot of boiling water. The Japanese, however, tell it differently. In their version, the first and second little pigs lose their houses but escape with their lives. They flee to the home of the third little pig, and the three of them work together to capture the wolf. The emphasis is on cooperation. Japanese children who have learned their lessons well point out that if the pigs had worked together in the first place to build one house, the problem could have been avoided.

These contrasting versions of the same story illustrate an important cultural difference: in Japan the group is always more important than the individual. At home children live in the limelight, the center of attention; that changes when they go out into the world. School is where children learn to work together, to be part of the group.

Regular school comes as a rude shock to small children who have been treated like princes and princesses by their mothers; therefore, many parents pay to send their children to preschool. About 40 percent of three-year-olds and 92 percent of four- and five-year-olds are enrolled in some kind of kindergarten. Like all Japanese schools, the classes are big—about thirty students to one teacher, usually a young woman trained in a junior college.

The main thing these young children learn is to be part of a group and not to stand out. But now some parents, looking down the road and seeing tough, competitive times ahead for their children, are beginning to wonder if the nonacademic approach is really the right one. Worried that their kids may not be able to keep up once they enter regular elementary school, these parents want to give their children a head start in academic subjects. Responding to that kind of pressure from parents, some schools are beginning to introduce reading and writing in kindergarten. Not everyone thinks that's a good idea.

I was invited to have lunch with the mothers at a private, church-run kindergarten in a small city. By then I was accustomed to the routine: I would meet a couple of teachers, drink green tea in the principal's office, make polite conversation, and wait to see what would happen next. What

I hoped for was a chance to be an observer. I wanted to watch children playing, to see if I could pick out any differences between American kids and Japanese kids of this age.

It was quiet; I thought the children must be outside. But I became aware of a rustling in the big empty room behind me. When I glanced around, I saw that the room was no longer empty; about fifty women were seated in rows. In front of them stood a microphone and a podium. I had a sudden rush of uneasiness.

"What is going on?" I asked.

"You will speak to them," said the director of the kindergarten, smiling gently.

"About what?"

"Early childhood education. Please speak for forty-five minutes."

But I couldn't speak for even five minutes on early childhood education. Uneasiness increased to anxiety. "What aspect of it?"

"This question: Is it better to foster creativity in young children or begin them on their academic path as early as possible?"

I did have an opinion on that, but I wanted to check out something first. "What is the philosophy of this school?" I asked.

"Encouraging creativity."

Thank goodness, I thought.

The mothers looked at me expectantly, waiting to hear what I had to say. I explained, through an interpreter, that I was not an educator. I had never taught school. I knew next to nothing about early childhood education either in Japan or in the United States. But I was definitely in favor of encouraging creativity.

While the interpreter translated, I tried frantically to think of what to say next. Everything that came to mind seemed like a platitude, so I asked them to help me out with questions. One stood up and asked how to teach creativity, something I suppose everyone would like to know. I said I thought creativity wasn't something that could be taught; maybe you can encourage it, or maybe you just allow it to happen and try not to get in the way. By the time I visited this kindergarten, I had found out that most Japanese teachers are defensive about the charge of Westerners that they stifle creativity. I had also observed that by the time children reach junior high school, spontaneity has been successfully trained out of them. The urge to do something original, something of one's own, has disappeared.

I rambled on for a while about definitions of success, about materialism, about all sorts of things until the forty-five minutes was up. The mothers collected their children and left, and a few women stayed to eat box lunches in the principal's office. The conversation continued for two more hours, mostly small talk, mostly in Japanese.

It was drizzling when we arrived at what had been described to me as an "experimental school," but nobody seemed to mind the dampness. Kids played in the wet sand, clambered over a jungle gym, scrambled up a fake mountain. Tiny pompon girls stopped dancing and hid when they saw me. As soon as I took out my camera I was immediately surrounded—taking pictures is a national mania, and a camera is the signal for kids to throng around, flashing bright grins and peace signs with such enthusiasm that you can't get a picture of them simply being themselves.

The tour was brief; it was time for the children to go home. We sat in the principal's office, sipping more green tea. Outside the window mothers and grandmothers arrived to collect the kindergartners. Many women had toddlers and babies with them; the mothers carried the smaller ones in their arms or pushed them in strollers, while the grand-mothers carried the babies the old-fashioned way, strapped to their backs. One father was in the group, and his presence caused comment in our room. Fathers traditionally have had little to do with child rearing, but that—like carrying a baby on one's back—is also changing.

This kindergarten was unusual because it was associated with the education department of a university; that affiliation granted it a certain amount of freedom to experiment. Moth-ers vied to get their youngsters into the school, and there were four times as many applicants as spaces available.

"How do you pick the children you'll admit?"

"We're looking for a creative spark," the principal said. He described the test: The children are given blocks to play with and a box to climb over, and from this the observers try to measure the degree of creativity. The test eliminates half the children; parents of the remaining applicants draw lots to determine who will be admitted. Mrs. Murata thinks drawing lots means the teachers don't rely completely on their own judgment but allow chance to play a role. It is probably also a face-saving device for disappointed mothers, who can blame fate, rather than a child's deficiency in "cre-ative spark," for success or failure in the long educational road ahead.

That long road includes nine years of compulsory edu-cation: six years of primary school and three years of junior high school; most students go on for three more years of high school.

The school year begins the first of April with a special ceremony. Confucian tradition makes ceremonies impor-tant, and there is more emphasis on starting school than on graduating. *Commencement* really does mean *beginning* in Japan, and commencement ceremonies are solemn events that emphasize the seriousness of the business of acquiring an education. The school year ends the following March. Summer vacation lasts only five or six weeks, from mid-July until early September. Japanese children also attend school on Saturday mornings. It sounds like a lot of school, and it is.

In the U.S. most school districts require a school year of 180 days, which includes a few days for trips, graduation ceremonies, and so on. The Japanese say their school year is 240 days—60 days longer than in the United States. But the difference is not as great as it seems. Only 210 days are required, and Saturday mornings are counted as full days. Then local school boards tack on an extra 30 days for field trips, sports days, cultural festivals, and other events. This works out to about 195 days of classroom instruction—still much more than in U.S. schools. Over a twelve-year period, it adds up to the equivalent of at least one year more than American students spend in school. Add to that the time Japanese students attend cram schools and enrichment courses of various kinds and you can see one reason why many people think Japanese education has an edge over American education: there's more of it.

But the methods are different, too, and here's where the controversy begins. Japanese education emphasizes the "mug-and-jug" approach: students are empty "mugs" into which the teacher, the "jug," pours information; the "mug" pours it out again on exams. This approach has been out of date for a long time in American education, where the emphasis is more likely to be on process—on using information, rather than just memorizing it.

Nevertheless, Japanese students have mastered the basics. Some Japanese students I met were amazed that American students couldn't locate Japan on a world map. I didn't tell them about a study showing that some American high school students couldn't even locate the United States on a world map. It's this kind of deficiency in American education that sends our experts scrambling to learn the secrets of the Japanese system.

Most of the curricula are what you'd expect to find in any school—reading, writing, and arithmetic—but there are some differences. In one first-grade music class, I saw children learning to sight-read. They sat at their desks with two-octave keyboards and blew air into a tube to make the sound. The music was propped up in front of them. The teacher played and sang a musical phrase, and the children sang with him; then they played the next phrase on their little keyboards. This musical training continues all through primary school for two hours a week—not only playing and singing, but also listening to Japanese classical music—as well as to Bach, Handel, and Beethoven.

"Moral education," as it's called, is taught for an hour a week in primary school—a highly structured hour built around twenty-eight themes that cover the attitudes, habits, and kinds of behavior valued by the Japanese. These include the importance of order, manners, respect for public property, endurance, justice, the individual's place in the group, harmony with nature, and so on. It's one part of the curriculum that doesn't use a textbook; educational television programs have been developed for moral education classes.

Several times a week everyone gathers outside the school for morning exercises before classes begin. Some primary schools have a lunch program, and everybody (including the teacher) eats in the classroom and eats the same thing; in other schools, children bring lunches from home. Cafeterias are rare. A ten-minute class meeting follows afternoon classes. Then the children stuff all their books and papers into their backpacks and scatter to school clubs, private lessons, or home.

Students spend about twenty minutes cleaning the hallways and classrooms, either after lunch or at the end of the day. I was never around when this was going on; it wasn't something they wanted to show honored guests. But I did see evidence of it: a rack covered with dozens of rags out behind the school. When a bell rings, kids stop playing and grab the rags and old-fashioned brooms and dusters. This daily cleaning, combined with shoes being left outside, means that the schools are spotless, graffiti unheard of.

Classes are large—the legal maximum is forty-five, but Monboshu, the Japanese Ministry of Education, plans to reduce the maximum to forty by 1991. Since children are not separated by ability, every class has a full range of students, from slow to superbright. The Japanese believe that everyone can learn all the material if they are willing to study hard. But every class has a share of students who are bored because they're falling behind—or because they're ahead of the rest.

According to a 1987 report by a task force from the U.S. Department of Education, Japanese classes are larger than American ones, but they are also more orderly. Students pay more attention and behave better, and when they move from one project to the next, they do it faster and more efficiently. As a result, the study claims, Japanese students spend about one-third more time during a typical class period actually *learning* than American students do—and this high level of discipline is achieved without the teacher exercising strong authority.

That's what the report says, but I heard a different story. American teachers who have taught in Japan tell tales and write articles about their classroom experiences, claiming that discipline can be quite harsh—or that many teachers simply make a deal with their students, allowing them to file their nails, gaze out the window, read magazines, or do whatever else they please as long as they don't disrupt the class and disturb other students who do want to learn.

Since in Japan nobody flunks out and nobody gets left back, students in each grade are all the same age. The rule is that even hopeless students are passed through the system, even though they fall further and further behind. Schools are required to follow the same curriculum, but that doesn't mean the quality of instruction is the same—everybody knows which are the top schools, the bottom schools, and all the levels in between. When students finish ninth grade, the third year of "lower secondary," they're allowed to leave school; not many do. Students must take exams for entrance into "upper secondary"—senior high school—but there is always some high school that will take even the poorest, least-motivated students. This guarantees that almost everybody graduates from high school.

Yashi

It was the first day of school after summer vacation, and clusters of kids in school uniforms crowded the streets. Most of the girls wore skirts and sailor blouses; the boys wore trousers and short-sleeved shirts; little children had identical hats. I was people-watching with a young teacher named Yashi at an outdoor cafe in the Harajuku section of Tokyo, an area of cafes and boutiques along tree-lined streets. There was more greenery and open space there than in most other parts of Tokyo; consequently it was fashionable and shockingly expensive, apartments renting for thousands of dollars a month. Elegantly dressed young women hurried by, looking like something out of a fashion magazine.

Yashi—from Yasushi—was his American nickname, picked up when he was a student at an American college.

Yashi is a graduate of Waseda, one of Japan's top private universities. He was smart enough to be admitted to the high school there, and that set him up for entrance to the university. After graduating from Waseda, he went to the United States for a year. Yashi studied both architecture and psychology, but neither was what he wanted to do for the rest of his life. And so now he teaches in a *yobiko*, a cram school for helping students to pass the university entrance exams, while he figures out what he really wants.

"What do you think of Japanese education?" Yashi asked.

I wasn't ready to answer his question then. I had been in Japan only a couple of days, and since school was just reopening after a five-week summer break, I hadn't visited any schools or talked with any kids or teachers. Japanese education was something I had only read about.

For the past few years, Americans have had a love affair with Japanese education, not only because of Japan's economic growth, which many believe is related to its educational system, but also because of the country's extremely high literacy rate (98 percent—especially impressive considering how difficult it is to learn to read *kanji*) and because of the high scores by Japanese youth on math and science tests. American writers and educators have spent time observing how the Japanese do it and trying to figure out how to pull off the same miracles in American schools.

But not everyone is enthralled with the Japanese system, based primarily on rote memorization. Still, there is good reason for this approach. When learning to read requires mastery of some two thousand separate characters, memorization is the only way to do it. Memorization is also important in studying any subject involving masses of data—history, for example, as well as science and math. But memorized data merely provide the information to work with; then independent thought, critical analysis, abstract reasoning, and creative imagination should take over. Critics say that's exactly where Japanese education falls down.

Memorization is a form of discipline, and discipline is highly prized by the Japanese. When Japanese universities test students for entrance, they're not interested in how well the applicant can think or how he can apply his knowledge; they're not interested in his creativity or his leadership abilities. They focus exclusively on the raw test scores that indicate how well the student has disciplined himself to absorb and retain huge masses of information. (I've used *he* because most university applicants are boys. There is much less pressure on girls for academic achievement.)

Yashi answered his own question bluntly. "Japanese education is declining sharply and rapidly," he said, "especially public education." What he sees instead is a rise in the quality and importance of private education.

He is not alone in his opinion. The Japanese generally are critical of their educational system. While the report by the U.S. Department of Education task force praises Japanese schools, Japan's National Council on Educational Reform is less positive, citing "the state of desolation" it sees in education. There are complaints that the principal goal of Japanese education is to prepare students to pass entrance examinations, to get them into the "right" high school, leading to the "right" university and then to a job with the "right" company. People complain, but no one wants to buck the system. It's a long road that starts when the child is very young, and it starts at home.

Education Mama

She is called *kyoiku mama* ("education mama"), and though she's often the butt of jokes, she's actually an important part of Japanese education. The child's education is the main focus of the family, and a mother's sense of accomplishment is linked to how well her children achieve in school. Many women believe their success as mothers is judged by their children's school performance, and they devote their lives to making sure their kids do well.

Mrs. Yoshida, whom I met in Tsukuba Science City, calls herself an education mama. Once a professional woman with a career, she now centers her life on her three children. She says she and her friends are always on the alert for special kinds of classes that might give their children an edge in the education race. The baby is still too young, but Mrs. Yoshida has enrolled her 3½-year-old daughter in a prenursery music class in which the teacher works with the children to develop a sense of rhythm and pitch that later will be translated into real music lessons. Next year, the girl will enter nursery school, and when she's five, she'll move on to kindergarten.

Mrs. Yoshida's son, nine, already has more pressure put on him—not because he's the oldest but because he's a boy. He attends an English conversation class a couple of times a week to keep up the language skills he acquired when the family lived abroad for six months. The older he gets, the more he will find himself spending whatever after-school time he has in *juku*, private tutoring schools. Some of this tutoring will be extra enrichment, like English conversation. But some will be cram courses to get him into a good high school—and still more cramming to get him into a good college.

As education mamas go, Mrs. Yoshida is low-key. The totally dedicated *kyoiku mama* works with her child every night, drilling him in memorization. She makes sure he has the best possible study conditions. In extreme cases, she might even go to school in his place if he is absent and take notes for him. His success—or failure—is his mother's.

106

School Trip: The Nature Center

It was a long drive from Utsunomiya, past rice fields ready for harvest and old farmhouses with thatched roofs, to the Minaminasu Children's Nature Center. Throughout the year, school trips and special events are carefully planned and highly organized to get the kids used to working together as a group and to identifying with their class and with their school. Taking a trip together to "enjoy nature" also teaches them to behave appropriately in public. But besides these lofty goals, the fourth, fifth, and sixth graders from Ōuichi Primary School were ready for a good time.

It was raining again, but I assumed there would be activities going on inside the center. First I had to meet the director, who, after the ritual green tea, stepped over to his desk and took out his watercolors and ink. In what seemed like a matter of seconds, he painted a picture of an iris to accompany a haiku, a seventeen-syllable poem usually about nature and the seasons. He painted one for me and one for Mrs. Murata. Then the head teacher of the visiting school came in, three uniformed staff members from the center were introduced, and everybody tried to figure out exactly what I wanted. I wanted to see some children, I said. They would arrange it, they promised.

But my idea of watching kids involved in a science project or playing games evaporated. About fifty pupils in matching shorts and shirts were lined up in a gymnasium on three rows of folding chairs facing a row of chairs for the visiting dignitaries. A videocamera whirred; snapshot cameras clicked as we went through more speeches and more introductions, with Mrs. Murata acting as interpreter.

"What kinds of things will you be doing here at the center?" I asked. Hands shot up; the children's teacher chose who would answer. One by one they rose and bowed, addressing me as "Meyer-san," and rattled off replies: "looking at the stars through a telescope," "enjoying nature," "having lunch together," "sleeping in the dormitory together," "taking a bath together." Mrs. Murata translated, making sure I didn't miss the point—that they liked to do things together. One boy said "campfire" so clearly that I recognized it as English; his classmates applauded.

When I invited them to ask me questions, nearly every hand was waving. We might have gone on all day with their curious questions: What do you like to eat? Do you like Japanese food? What does your house look like? What is your neighborhood like? What sports do American children like? Do American children like nature? What kinds of insects do you have in America? They asked personal questions, too: How old are you? Do you believe in God?

Each listened respectfully to my reply and sat down, and then the next child popped up. At the end, they rushed forward to shake my hand. Their teacher explained that I was the first *gaijin* they had met.

Kurabane Primary School

A spectacular stuffed peacock spreads its shimmering tail at one end of the principal's office, where the school photographer lined us up for the official photograph. The Kurabane Primary School is one of the oldest in the country, located on an old samurai road, the principal said, with the samurai gate still there. I couldn't see the gate—rain was coming down in torrents—but the ceiling of the room where we met was paneled in old wood, although the building itself was quite new.

School architecture in Japan is usually dreary and generally uniform: rectangular concrete buildings two or three stories high, with all the rooms opening onto an outside hallway. The rooms are rectangular and crowded with double desks, each shared by two pupils. Everyone faces the blackboard at the front of the room. The Japanese don't go in for decorating classrooms, or even for such basic comforts as heat and air conditioning. Students swelter through humid summers and endure the chill of winters. Katherine, the Japanese Exchange and Teaching Program teacher who came along with us that day, told me that the room heaters aren't turned on in most schools until December 15. She wears three layers of clothing and marvels that the children aren't as miserable as she is. This is part of the discipline that is supposed to "harden" Japanese students.

Katherine whispered that the teacher of the sixth-grade social studies class we were visiting was unusual in the way he related to his students—there was no "mug-and-jug" philosophy operating in his classes. The lesson for the day was on the Edo period, and the class was working on the relationship between samurai and peasant. The teacher wrote on the board that 85 percent of the population during that period were peasants, and 7 percent were samurai. "How is it," he asked (Mrs. Murata translated for me), "that 85 percent of the people could be controlled by 7 percent of the people?"

"This is remarkable," Katherine whispered in my other ear. "Teachers never ask pupils questions like that."

Hands flew up, and the teacher pointed to one of the students. The boy stood up, bowed, answered, and sat down. (Mrs. Murata didn't translate his explanation.)

"How many agree?" the teacher asked. Those who did raised their left hands, thumb and forefinger forming a circle for the "okay" sign. Everybody agreed.

When the bell rang at 2:50, the pupils scrambled to get their book bags and returned to their seats. Then, sitting at their desks after their brief class meeting, they sang "Eidelweiss," from *The Sound of Music*, in English. These students wouldn't begin studying English until the following year, and I was made to understand that they had gone to quite a lot of effort to learn this for my benefit. At the end they stood, made a low bow to the teacher, and chorused *"Konnichi-wa"* ("Good afternoon").

Bedlam followed dismissal. Usually the children are expected to stay for at least two hours to take part in club activities. From fourth grade on, pupils choose a club every April when school begins—calligraphy, art, crafts, sports, drama, needlework. But it was raining so hard that the groups that normally met outside were jammed into the big gym, some shooting baskets, some going through a drill routine for the school sports day. I got out my little camera and tried to get a few shots of all the activity, but as soon as they spotted the camera they were right in front of my lens, jostling each other, wagging peace signs, swarming over Katherine and me.

We raced to the safety of the principal's office and hid out until it was time for the "meeting." This meeting with hand-picked students, all "delegates" of some sort, took place in almost every school I visited. My request to "talk with some of the students" was inevitably highly structured. I always hoped for an informal handful with only an interpreter present, but it never seemed to work out that way.

All these delegates wore tags with their names typed in both *kanji* and *romaji*. The questions were so readily forthcoming and so thoughtful that I wondered how carefully the students had been coached: How did you become a writer? How many pages a day do you write? How long does it take to write a book? What happens if you are late with your manuscript? When that subject was exhausted, they moved on to questions about American schooling—how long vacations were, whether or not American kids had homework over the summer holiday. They groaned at my answers, a glimpse of lives less structured than theirs.

When they ran out of questions, I wrote my name for them on the blackboard, in script and in block letters. They have not yet begun to study English, and I realized that it must look as exotic and incomprehensible to them as their names did to me in *kanji*. They rose, bowed together, said *"Konnichi-wa"* in unison, and crowded around to present their name tags as *meishi*.

Juku

Since the Japanese school system operates on the theory that everyone should be able to keep up with the work in each course, there are no "gifted" programs for very bright students and no special classes for students with learning problems. *Juku*, a Japanese phenomenon, fill the gaps.

Thousands of *juku*, special schools that are privately owned and operated for profit, offer enrichment to those who want it and remedial help to those who need it. There are both academic and nonacademic *juku*. Younger kids are usually enrolled in nonacademic schools for instruction in abacus, calligraphy, and other subjects. But academic *juku*, which are a way of life for students from junior high school through high school, are deadly serious. *Yobiko*, which specializes in preparation for university entrance examinations, is a type of *juku*.

There are all kinds and sizes of *juku*, ranging from one-room operations to big chains with large faculties and huge enrollments. One major chain has more than a million students scattered at branches throughout the country. But the one-room school with one teacher is the most common.

Because education is taken so seriously, *juku* are big business in Japan, comprising one of the major growth industries. A little more than 6 percent of all first graders are in some sort of *juku*. By ninth grade, the average has climbed to more than 47 percent—higher in the cities, lower out in the country. During the first eight years, most kids in *juku* are simply trying to keep up with the breakneck pace of regular school. But by ninth grade they're worried about getting into a good high school, and the extra studies are aimed at passing the difficult high school entrance exams.

Since so many kids go to *juku*, few complain much about it. Their friends are all at *juku* on Saturday afternoons, after school, and during the evenings, so they might as well be there too. Some people claim the *juku* are in fact better than the public schools, because *juku* are free to use different educational approaches and may give much more individual attention to their students. Since the *juku* industry is highly competitive, most *juku* owners are motivated to help their students. By improving their students' schoolwork, they improve their own reputations, get more students, and make more money.

Some critics say *juku* operators are more interested in profits than in education. Nevertheless, their popularity points up a failure of the Japanese public school system: most students don't get what they need in regular school and must pay to get it elsewhere.

One of the basic principles of Japanese education is that it is egalitarian, that everyone has an equal opportunity. The son of a poor laborer supposedly has the same chance as the son of a banker of getting into a good high school, which will lead to acceptance at a top national university, which in turn will lead to being hired by the government or a major corporation. In reality, only those who can afford to send their children to expensive *juku* are likely to wind up on the winning track.

I spent an hour at a *juku*, a Saturday afternoon class for primary school children on abacus techniques, and left understanding more about the best results of Japanese education.

The Japanese word for this ancient device for doing arithmetic calculations is *soroban;* we call it an abacus. The abacus these children were using had ten parallel wires strung on a frame, nine beads on each wire. The beads on each wire have the same value—a value of one on the first wire on the right, of ten on the second wire, and of one hundred on the third. Numbers are added or subtracted by moving the beads on each wire.

The class was held in a crowded, stuffy room and taught by a high school math teacher who "moonlights" by operating his own one-room *juku*. The teacher explained that his students were grouped by ability, not by age, and so the range in this class ran from his seven-year-old daughter to twelve- and thirteen-year-olds. The pupils hunched over their *soroban*, held in one hand, manipulating the beads with the thumb and index finger of the other hand. The teacher rapidly read off a series of four-digit numbers for them to add. They had the total the moment he finished reading. Work sheets drilled them in multiplication and division, as well as addition and subtraction of gigantic numbers.

This teacher believes in the discipline of "mental training." The next exercise was to run three- and four-digit numbers mentally, without actually using the abacus. Visualizing an imaginary abacus in the palm of their hands, they moved imaginary counters to come up with the answers. Next he turned on a TV monitor; two-digit numbers flashed on the screen as fast as I could read them, and the pupils added them up in their heads. I lost track by the third number, when the total had reached only eighty-nine, but the children continued on with lightning speed and arrived at the total as the last number hit the screen. Even the youngest of them could handle numbers as easily as I recite the alphabet. It's in activities like this that Japanese students shine.

8

More and More Rules, Less and Less Freedom

If It's Monday, It Must Be Pink

"**M**onday they must pack a pink cloth napkin in their lunch boxes. Tuesday it's blue, Wednesday green, Thursday pink again, and Friday back to blue."

Mrs. Saitō grumbles about the silly rule. "My son is never quite sure which color he is supposed to have in his lunch that day, so he keeps all three napkins at school rather than risk not having the right one. After a few weeks the napkins are very dirty, but he doesn't want to bring them home for me to wash because he's afraid he won't take the right color the next time."

Mrs. Saitō has talked to other parents about the napkin rule. Some of them agree with her that it's meaningless and causes needless problems, just one more rule among the dozens that begin to mount up in junior high school. But others are adamant, claiming it's an important discipline and that students have to learn to follow rules. Following rules is important in Japanese society, and the place to learn is in school.

One of the basic rules in most junior and senior high schools (called "lower and upper secondary schools") is the school uniform. At one time all students, even in university, had to wear uniforms. Now universities have given them up; most junior and senior highs still require them, but even that is no longer universal. When the subject comes up, as it often does, the school authorities make the final decision. School regulations also cover hairstyles and accessories. In some schools the hair must be cut a certain length; in others, girls who want longer hair must wear it in braids, and until their hair is long enough to braid, they must divide it in two sections and fasten it with rubber bands. Permanents are not allowed. Makeup is forbidden, and so is jewelry: no rings, no bracelets, no earrings. Skirt length and fingernail length are both subject to regulation. Inspections are held monthly.

Gina, the Canadian exchange student, remembers her first inspection. Her fingernails didn't pass, but the teacher didn't just say they were too long and tell her to cut them. Instead, the teacher cut Gina's nails for her!

A nineteen-year-old student, Takeshi Hayashi, was so annoyed by the oppressive regulations when he was on a school trip in high school that he decided to write a book about the strict regulations of some high schools. A teacher caught one of Takeshi's friends wearing pants a few centimeters narrower than allowed and called the boy's mother long-distance to inform her of the infraction. When the trip was over, Takeshi checked the regulations at other schools and discovered all kinds of trivial rules: some schools forbade students to wear mufflers, others forbade girls to wear sweaters. The book is enormously popular among students who detest the rules.

116

All these rules are supposed to show students that school is serious business and that discipline is paramount. The emphasis on academic subjects increases, and so does the "mug-and-jug" routine of filling a student with factual knowledge.

Junior high students carry heavy course loads. They review the thousand *kanji* characters they learned in elementary school and memorize another thousand, so that after nine years of school they have acquired basic literacy. They work on the history and geography of both Japan and the rest of the world. By ninth grade, they've added a study of Japanese government, with attention to economic systems. In math they cover algebra, plane and solid geometry, probability and statistics. And so it goes, through a tough and demanding curriculum that includes fine arts and music (they sing in choruses and play in ensembles, and study classical Japanese and Western music), physical education, industrial arts, and homemaking.

And they study English. Technically English is an elective, but that doesn't mean students have a choice in the matter. The principal of the school "elects" the foreign language the students in his school will study, and almost invariably that language is English, because it is required on university entrance exams. Each year students add about 350 words to their vocabulary, study grammar, and memorize basic sentence patterns in which to fit the vocabulary and some idioms.

Mother Goose and Androcles

A parade of girls in school uniforms marched down the aisle of the school auditorium and up the steps to the stage. While a piano played "London Bridge Is Falling Down," they lined up in front of the curtain. Out from the wings swept the star, Mother Goose, who introduced the others: the pussycat, the queen, Hector Protector, Mary and her lamb, Humpty Dumpty—quite a long cast of characters. Each one bowed and said or did something, like a second-grade production in an American elementary school. But this was the seventh-grade English class. They had been studying English for about six months and were barely intelligible; the wonder of it was that they could do it at all.

At the break, after two run-throughs, their American teacher led a shy Mother Goose over to me and asked if I would go over her part with her. Her script had been doctored to eliminate some of the words that were too difficult for anyone at her level to get her tongue around: *thoroughly*, for example, with both a *th* and an *l*. She read the script once and then did it from memory. She had memorized it perfectly; the problem was pronunciation. At the next rehearsal, I thought I understood it much better—but by then I had nearly memorized it myself.

In another production, the eleventh graders had put up a clever set in just a few minutes—a village with two neighboring "houses" made of boxes. Two characters peered out of "windows" cut in the boxes; they were the lovers. Other characters made their entrances—a greedy uncle, a captain of the guard, a slave, and a lion, played by a girl with a long tail pinned to the skirt of her uniform. The rehearsal of *Androcles and the Lion* got under way.

It was two weeks before the performance, and things were still ragged. The actors were blowing lines and missing cues, but they worked hard to pronounce their words and make themselves heard in the back of the auditorium. They managed well most of the time, although sometimes it was hard to understand them. Their audience for the performance would be primarily their mothers, most of whom didn't speak English. I was probably the severest critic they would ever have.

"Praise them lavishly, will you?" their teacher begged.

I did. I fibbed a little and told them I understood every word.

A Question of Hobbies

Hobby was a word that came up often, although it's not one you hear much in the United States. At one school during the usual meeting, the students all introduced themselves by name, age, and hobby: cooking, music (one classical, one pop), sports. What they didn't mention was watching television, although that is what most kids do with their free time—the little of it there is.

Television seems to be every bit as much of an addiction in Japan as it is in America, and the programming is often just as mindless. One night in a tiny hotel room I watched a strange kind of "Candid Camera" in which men were made-up elaborately and concealed in unlikely places—one was covered in artificial flowers and stretched out flat on his back in a public garden, another installed as part of a relief map of Japan. The idea was to startle passersby, always women and young girls, who reacted with shrieks and giggles. Another time I stayed with a family whose after-dinner plans every Friday evening included watching "Survival Game," in which junior high students run wild obstacle courses.

Japan has a reputation for being a nation of readers, devouring vast quantities of newspapers, books, magazines, and comic books. English titles give a clue to the contents of some specialized magazines: *Peter*, the "Cat Culture Magazine for Women"; *Nan Da*, the "Magazine for Aggressive

119

Women"; *With*, the "Culture Magazine for Your Life." There were maybe a half-dozen magazines for teenage girls, including *Olive*, the "Magazine for Romantic Girls," which in its September issue featured an article on how to use a knife and fork European-style. The male equivalents include *Hot Dog, Brutus, Tarzan,* and *Popeye*.

I spent hours one day talking about books with a woman who translates young adult novels from English to Japanese. Mrs. Kakegawa's specialty is the work of Virginia Hamilton. She likes Hamilton's themes but has to struggle with translation because of the author's use of sentence fragments which are difficult to render in Japanese. Translation is always a tricky undertaking, and not all of the problems are because of language. Sometimes cultural differences get in the way. In Japan a serious idea must be seriously expressed, Mrs. Kakegawa told me; the use of humor in a serious book is considered inappropriate. And anything having to do with sex is out. She objects to Judy Blume's books, for instance, because the themes have to do with the discovery of sexuality. In Japan junior high school students do not date, nor do most senior high school students.

We had read many of the same books for young people, but our reactions to them were quite different. *The Stone-Faced Boy*, by Paula Fox, was one of her favorites, so I suggested *Julie of the Wolves*, by Jean Craighead George. "Too journalistic," she said. Then I mentioned one of my favorite authors, Katherine Paterson; I cry every time I read *Bridge to Terabithia*. I thought the sad ending would appeal to Japanese readers. "Too emotional," Mrs. Kakegawa said.

Meiji Welcomes Mrs. Meyer

I almost didn't get there. I had been invited to attend Sports Day, honoring the fortieth anniversary of Meiji Junior

High School and originally scheduled for Friday. But on Friday the rains came, and the event was postponed until the following Monday; could I come then instead? I checked the complicated schedule Mrs. Murata and her colleagues had worked out for me; there seemed to be no time. Mrs. Murata thought otherwise. "It's important," she said. "You must go. I will work out the rest of it."

And so on a hot, sunny Monday at noon, we drove to the junior high school in a "bed town" or bedroom community about a half hour outside of Utsunomiya. Cars were lined up all along the road leading to the school, but a place had been saved for us in the inner parking lot. Everyone was gathered out on the athletic field; the program had started at nine, and a parents' group was busy judging the fancy-dress parade. Canvas shelters had been set up next to the field for spectators. Dressed in a white jogging suit, the principal came out to greet me and show me to my seat. That's when I saw the huge banner strung along the side of the building, white letters on a blue background: MRS. CAROLYN MEYER WELCOME TO MEIJI JUNIOR HIGH SCHOOL.

The principal led me out onto the field and pointed to an old American flag, with forty-eight stars, that had been run up the flagpole. While we all gazed at the Stars and Stripes, someone turned on the record player and "The Star-Spangled Banner" blared out over the PA system. I'd never had anything like this happen before, and I was deeply moved.

A rickety wooden platform not much bigger than my kitchen table was set up on the field with a microphone. I managed to climb up the shaky steps, followed by two girls wearing their stiff paper costumes for the fancy-dress parade. The girls presented me with a bouquet of flowers, a handmade basket, and a brightly colored mat. They scrambled down again, and the principal asked me to address the students and their parents.

121

In such situations it helps to know that most people don't understand a word of what you're saying. Nevertheless, I thanked them for inviting me, congratulated them on their fortieth anniversary, and told them how touched I was to see my flag and hear my national anthem. I bowed and clambered down off the platform.

We sipped green tea and watched hundreds of students perform drills and exercises and group dances. Acrobats formed a human pyramid and did balancing acts. Then Mrs. Murata and I were invited to run in a lottery race. We lined up with other adults, someone fired a starting gun, we grabbed envelopes with a number inside (mine was number seven) and raced about twenty feet to a row of numbered bins. My number seven won me a pair of rubber gloves for washing dishes. Someone from the parents' group rushed over with another gift—a big bundle of *kampyo*, a kind of dried gourd used to make a certain type of sushi. It was time to leave; I said good-bye to the principal and other dignitaries. Mrs. Murata reminded me that I had to say good-bye to the students, too. So there I was again, clutching flowers, basket, mat, rubber gloves, and *kampyo*, bowing this way and that. Everyone clapped and clapped.

"You bow so nicely," Mrs. Murata said approvingly, and we took off for our next appointment.

Family Business

The motto of Sakushin Gakuin is One Family, One School. And this school was definitely a family business. Sakushin Gakuin may be the largest high school in Japan, with eight thousand students—forty-five hundred boys and thirty-five hundred girls—not counting the elementary school, junior high school, and two-year junior college for girls. The day of my visit there was a ground-breaking ceremony for a new building that would be part of a four-year college to open soon.

Mrs. Funada, an elegant woman in a saffron-yellow dress and cobalt-blue jewelry greeted us in her fifth-floor office with its view of Utsunomiya and the mist-shrouded mountains in the distance. Sakushin Gakuin was founded in 1885; they were still talking about their centennial and showed me a videotape made in observance of it. Mrs. Funada is the widow of the grandson of the school's founder. There is a tradition in the Funada family of serving in the Diet, the governing body of Japan, and Mrs. Funada's son both carries on that tradition and helps to run the school.

Instead of green tea, there were glasses of cold English tea. Mr. Ōshima, the head English teacher, presented me with a history of the school, two inches thick, in Japanese. Then the school photographer appeared for the formal group portraits. For the next three hours, he followed us everywhere, and some of my snapshots show him taking pictures of me taking pictures of him.

My tour of the school was well organized and efficient, starting with a visit to the design department, which was part of the engineering department, which in turn belonged to the technical school. The technical school was on a lower academic level than the rest of the school, which was on a university track. Technical students assume they will go directly into the work force after graduation, although some in the design department hope to go on to art school. Those who hit the job market with only a high school education may have problems. Because the demand by industry for senior high graduates has dropped off, many students decide to attend some kind of specialized school for a year before they start looking for a job.

In the drafting room students worked on designs for a

camping shelter. One boy showed us his idea for under-water camping gear. On the top floor of another building students sat at computer terminals, entering commands in English. The computer mainframe was in a separate room, the only part of the school (except for the principal's office and a small reception room) that was air-conditioned. Every-one was sweltering.

We had fallen behind in our agenda, and we arrived late at the class for the tea ceremony. The teacher who was waiting for us outside the classroom was a Filipino-American from Chicago named Holly. Her Oriental features fooled me at first, and I was surprised by her American accent. "We were wondering what happened to you!" she said.

A dozen or so girls in school uniforms knelt quietly on *tatami* and another half-dozen were preparing the tea. Most teachers dress conservatively in somber colors and wear no jewelry, but this group's teacher wore an ivory necklace and a dramatic silver pin in the shape of a dragonfly. "She's an English teacher," Holly whispered, "but she won't speak English to me. She uses the excuse that I understand Japanese."

First came a plate of dainty sweets made of bean paste and formed into flower shapes, served on small wooden plates with tiny wooden spears for eating. Then the girls served the tea. Mr. Ōshima knelt properly throughout with-out moving. The kneeling girls looked uncomfortable. Holly and I didn't even try.

When the tour was over, I had a few minutes alone with Holly and another American teacher named Todd. Holly described her relationship with her students. She wears bright clothes—that day a red dress printed with sprigs of flowers—and she encourages her students to speak up, to ask questions, to respond in class.

"But that's not at all the way they have been trained,"

124

she said. "They have a hard time doing that. I can see them close down as they get older. When I work in the elementary school with the little children, they're very open and responsive, but by the time they're in junior high, they've begun to shut down."

"And by the time they're in senior high, it's all over," Todd added. "It's almost impossible to get them to open up. They won't explore new ideas. They've forgotten how to respond spontaneously." (Later, Gina explained why. "If you ask a question in class," she said, "the teacher tells you to shut up.")

Then we went out for lunch—Mr. Ōshima, Holly, Todd, and I. We went to a French restaurant, a treat for me because I was craving Western food. It was excellent, but in keeping with Japanese custom and appetites, the portions were minuscule: a single scallop in the middle of a puddle of green sauce, followed by the main course—three slices of beef the size of half-dollars. While we nibbled at each course, I got to know the teachers. Todd, whose Japanese wife had recently given birth to their first child, talked about his family. They had named the baby James. Many Japanese-American couples named their babies Ken, which can be written in Japanese characters. But they were afraid that when their son would later join other large groups of Japanese-Americans, he'd find that everyone had the same name.

Acts of Diplomacy

Mr. Kawahara, from the board of education office, tried to find a diplomatic way to ask me to be diplomatic. I had recently spent an afternoon at Utsunomiya Girls' High School, the most prestigious high school in the prefecture, and now I was on my way to a school ranked several notches lower. Seiryō Senior High School suffers from an inferiority complex because everyone knows it is not one of the best schools, and Mr. Kawahara wanted to make sure I wouldn't say anything to rub it in. It struck me as odd that he was afraid I or any visitor would be so tactless.

The reason the school doesn't rank higher is because it's relatively new: there hasn't been time to establish a track record of getting graduates into good universities, so the school does not attract highly competitive students who have set their sights on top schools. The students who end up there are those for whom such achievement is not a goal. It's a cycle that's hard to break.

The school was unusually quiet on the day I went to Seiryō; when Mrs. Murata pulled into the parking lot, we could see a group of students in one classroom, but all the other rooms looked empty. It turned out that the school was closed that day. The annual school festival had been held over the weekend, and both students and teachers were exhausted from the extra time and effort. Everyone had taken the day off, except for the group of students and a handful of teachers who agreed to come meet me.

The principal and four teachers lined up in the large entry hall, its floors waxed to a high polish; one pair of slippers perched at the edge of the step. We shuffled toward the principal's office and I presented my *meishi, Voices of South Africa*. They all had papers in front of them, and I realized the papers were copies of my résumé. When I had first contacted Jackson Bailey about visiting Japan, I had sent him a list of books and articles I'd written and other projects I'd been involved in—a rather detailed summary of a lifetime of work. Bailey apparently had sent a copy to Mrs. Murata, who copied it again and sent it to all the schools I was to visit. Everywhere I went that résumé showed up; if I didn't actually see it, I guessed from the conversation that they knew a lot more about me than I knew about them. But sometimes the résumé led to interesting conversations. At Seiryō it was a help. One of the teachers was doing special research on the Amish, a religious sect in Pennsylvania. I had grown up in Pennsylvania, and one of my early books was about the Amish. We had something in common to talk about.

Ceremonial small talk finished, we went to the room where the students waited. Someone remembered to put a vase of fresh flowers next to me. One of the English teachers sat on my left, the other on my right, notebooks open, ready to translate.

It seemed at first that absolutely nothing was going to happen. If I had been faced with such a situation in an American high school, I simply would have decided it wasn't worth pushing it any longer and called it quits. But that's not the way it works in Japan. I had learned that given enough time, students eventually loosen up and ask a few questions. So I waited, taking my cue from the teachers. I stayed at Seiryō for almost three hours, slowly working toward some kind of rapport with the students who, I knew, would much rather be somewhere else on their day off.

Their questions were not unusual, but at least they were asked: What did I think of English instruction in Japanese schools? How are French and Spanish taught in American schools? The students were interested in any comparisons I could make between Japanese education and American education—how much homework, how many vacations, whether or not students wore uniforms.

All of it seemed unremarkable to me, but it must have made an impression, because three months after my visit I got a note from one of the teachers: "You gave our students very important influence," he wrote. "One of our students who talked with you made a speech in English referring to

127

you. He got the first-place victory and he will be sent to Canada next summer for six weeks."

"What kind of hobbies do American students have?" someone asked. I mentioned rock music as the universal hobby, and then added, "Hanging out."

"Hanging out?" one of the teachers asked, looking up from his notes.

I tried to describe the great American pastime.

Then the teachers got into it. "What does it mean, 'A rolling stone gathers no moss'?"

I fumbled through an explanation, apparently not making it much clearer.

"Is it a good thing or a bad thing to be a rolling stone?" one of them asked.

Finally the session ended, the students left, and the teachers and I went back to the principal's office for coffee and debriefing. They remarked that there had been a number of American teachers around to visit their school on "fact-finding missions," but that the students had not been as open and responsive with them.

"Getting kids to talk in a group is like pulling teeth," I said.

"Pulling teeth? What does that mean, 'pulling teeth'?"

The Life of a Senior High School Student

In the library of International House in Tokyo I found a series of pamphlets describing the lives of Japanese schoolchildren, supposedly written by children and published by the International Society for Educational Information, a program for disseminating accurate information about Japan to other countries. The author of *The Life of a Senior High School Student* is anonymous, but sounds real enough as he describes his life and compares it to the lives of other Japanese

128

students. He says he attends a state university–affiliated senior high school, "an institution that pursues progressive educational methods" like having a two-semester system (most high schools operate on three semesters), not requiring school uniforms, and having an "absolute evaluation" of grades at the end of the semester.

In the "absolute" system, anyone scoring above a certain level gets a five; those below it, a one. There is always fear of receiving a one—failure—and the school rules state that even a single one means failure. (This policy seems meaningless, however, since if you go to school at all, you're automatically promoted to the next class.) Some schools have the "relative evaluation" system, in which grades from five to one are distributed according to percentages of the class, with five going to the top 10 percent of students, one to the lowest 10 percent, and other grades distributed on a curve.

The school term begins in April, and sometime in May the second-year students—juniors, eleventh graders—go off on an overnight hiking trip together. After exams in July, summer vacation begins. Second-year students go to a mountain dormitory owned by the school and spend several days experiencing "life with nature" and life without modern conveniences. Then in November there's a class trip to Kyoto and Nara. The pamphlet author points out that the traditional school excursion is not a pleasure trip, but "travel to acquire knowledge," aimed at acquainting students with their country by going places they don't normally visit. Plans for the November trip begin in the spring, with special lectures each week on ancient Japanese art, literature, and religion so students will know what they're seeing when they get there.

I've never seen anything quite like Japanese groups traveling to acquire knowledge. Nikko is a beautiful area of

129

shrines and temples not far from Utsunomiya. Some local people took me on a three-hour drive to see the spectacular waterfalls and breathtaking mountain vistas so acclaimed in my guidebook. But on the afternoon of our trip, everything was socked in with fog so thick that we could see only a few yards ahead of us. The next morning I was free to visit the temples and shrines on my own, although the Japanese were frankly unconvinced that anyone would actually *prefer* to go sightseeing alone.

I tried to get there early, but I wasn't early enough. The tour buses had arrived, and thousands of Japanese sight-seers, all in groups, had already descended. Schoolchildren in identical hats followed a teacher carrying a bright flag with a number on it. They clung together in close forma-tion—nobody wandered away from the group—and listened to the teacher's lecture. There were large groups of elderly people, also wearing matching hats and badges and also following a leader with a flag, and somewhat less organized groups of middle-aged men in business suits.

The place was jammed with people traveling to acquire knowledge; I was obviously the only tourist there alone. I spent about half an hour fighting my way to such main attractions as the three monkeys carved in a wooden panel above a temple doorway (See No Evil, Speak No Evil, Hear No Evil). And then I fled, to a tiny temple apparently not on anyone's required list. The only people there were a couple of women in straw hats, down on their hands and knees pulling weeds.

In *The Life of a Senior High School Student*, the author, a junior, describes his courses. He studies modern Japanese literature, Japanese and Chinese classics, and English—four hours of reading and one of composition. His class reads the works of well-known English authors rewritten in simple form: George Orwell's *Animal Farm* and Dickens's *A Christmas Carol*, for example. The five hours of instruction in math the students get each week don't seem to be enough to cover the subjects: differential and integral calculus, vector and matrix. Social studies covers the ancient and premodern periods of both Japanese history and world history before the Industrial Revolution. Memorization of dates, names, and facts is the name of the game.

All second-year students, who had chemistry and biology in their first year of high school, now study physics; third-year students study earth and space science. But, the author notes, there isn't much laboratory experimentation in his high school, partly because of the lack of lab equipment and partly because there's so much material to be covered in lectures that no time is left for lab work.

The serious lack of public parks and recreational facilities in Japanese cities makes physical education especially important. Boys have four hours of physical education; girls, two hours—plus two hours of home economics. There is some controversy about the policy of giving girls but not boys the two hours of domestic science. This is not so much a feminist argument as a contention that since Japanese men travel and sometimes have to survive alone overseas without anyone to look after them, they need to be able to take care of themselves, to sew on buttons and fix simple meals. University students away from home face the same problems, but they don't think that's a good enough reason to give up two hours of sports each week to learn to do "women's work."

Participation in school clubs is optional; some students don't join any, others join two, choosing from sports clubs, orchestra, chorus, opera clubs, and so on—all run by students. Clubs meet after school several times a week. Those who are involved seem to enjoy them, but many seniors I talked to had had to drop out. There simply was no time for clubs when most were already enrolled in *yobiko*, the cram schools for the dreaded university entrance exams.

Most Japanese high school students are actually forbidden to hold part-time jobs. Parents and educators believe students should spend their time studying. This is different in the United States, where about 63 percent of high school students over sixteen have some kind of part-time job. Some high school students asked me why Americans allowed it. I said we believe that jobs give teenagers a sense of responsibility, as well as a source of income—and with that, a certain amount of independence that Japanese teenagers don't have.

Japanese students get an allowance from their parents. In his pamphlet, the author reports that his parents give him ¥7000 a week—about fifty dollars—a high figure by our exchange rate, but not particularly high in Japanese terms. He spends half and saves the other half to buy a video deck, which he thinks will cost about ¥150,000. Saving money is a Japanese custom: people put away an average of 20 percent of their income, while Americans have a hard time squirreling away even 3 to 4 percent.

"Examination Hell"

There's a saying in Japan—"Sleep four, pass; sleep five, fail"—that gives an indication of how much time and effort go into preparing for "examination hell," or "exam wars" as it's variously called. Entrance exams color every aspect of the life of a student who wants to go to college. This one fact makes the lives of Japanese students totally different from the lives of most American students. Exams are said to get harder each year, and senior high schools try to persuade universities to stop putting excessively tough problems on the tests. But the universities insist that high academic requirements are absolutely necessary.

There are two sets of exams. The first, given in January, is a general test for all prospective entrants. Those who get a grade average above a certain point qualify for the second-stage exams in early March. Each university has its own passing point and gives its own exam.

Entrance exams come in two parts, compulsory and elective. Math, English, and Japanese are the compulsory subjects; elective subjects, like science and social studies, depend on the course of study the student plans to pursue in college. Once the decision is made, there's no turning back: students can't change majors, and they can't transfer to another university—unless they take the exams again and start over as freshmen.

American author Thomas P. Rohlen describes the tests in his book *Japan's High Schools*. "Much of the social studies part of entrance examinations seems like nothing more than a giant trivia contest compiled by scholars instead of popular culture freaks," he writes. Math and science are "quite straightforward and impressive." But the English section is something else. The emphasis there is on comprehension, and students are expected to translate into Japanese a sentence like this one: "With the continuous decrease, during the past few decades, in the length of the working day, recreation, or leisure time activity, has become a social problem of vital importance and one that has engaged the interest of many investigators."

Students who fail the exams for the school they want to attend sometimes spend a full year—and maybe more—preparing to take the exams again. Called *ronin*—after the "lordless wandering samurai"—they sometimes enroll in a full-time *yobiko*. About one out of four students taking the exams is *ronin,* and he may be taking them for the third or fourth time. Not many girls go to *yobiko*—male *ronin* outnumber females more than ten to one. Fewer than 25 percent of university students are women. But the number is increasing, although most women know their chances of achieving a professional career are slim.

Everybody complains about "examination hell," but nobody does anything about it. Most people agree publicly that the examinations are a bad thing and should be changed, that too much pressure is put on teenagers to spend their lives studying. But when it comes down to it, parents do everything possible to help their children gain a competitive edge. There is a lot of talk about changing this part of Japanese life, but not much happens. If the government does put pressure on national universities to restructure their examinations, people say the private universities will have all the prestige.

According to Thomas Rohlen, employers are impressed by the school's reputation rather than by the grades a student earns there. Thus, entrance exams are the most direct route to success—some would say the only route. The reason so many people study so hard to enter top universities is not to get a better education, but to get a better job after they graduate.

Conversation in a Coffeehouse

I thought I had seen enough high school festivals, but Mrs. Kahata—Mrs. Murata's friend in the city of Mito—had other ideas. On a Saturday morning, she drove me to Mito First High School. Mrs. Kahata has a particular interest in this school: her husband is a graduate, and the one thing that would make her most happy would be to have her oldest son follow in his father's footsteps. Like most Japanese, she believes that if only he could be motivated to apply himself, he would make the grades to go to his father's school. "I know once he got there, he'd enjoy it," she said.

Ten years ago the boys and girls of Mito First decided they didn't want to wear uniforms, and they convinced the administration to go along with that decision. Even more remarkable to me was the sight of boys and girls actually working together. In most schools the sexes stay separate, the girls clinging together in groups, the boys in their groups peering at the girls as if they were a different species altogether. But here the boys and girls had joint projects, one group making *mochi* (rice that had been boiled, pounded, and formed into balls), another showing a video they had made during their summer vacation.

The class had cooperated on writing a script that had gone through many changes before it was shot and edited. The story had to do with an arranged marriage. The young man already had a sweetheart and resisted the arrangement, but the two families were determined: one sold *natto*, fermented soybeans, and one sold rice—the perfect economic marriage, as well as a traditional Japanese food combination. The sweetheart's father was a baker, and the combination of bread and *natto* wouldn't work. If I followed it right, the rice seller's daughter eventually bowed out, leaving her lover to find happiness with the baker's daughter. The upbeat Western-style ending with the couple living happily ever after seemed very un-Japanese. Maybe this is changing, and in the future true love will triumph over familial duty.

Instead of passive exhibits, which I had seen in several other school festivals, these students had focused on game shows—the more raucous, the better. In the vast, echoing gymnasium the English-Speaking Society enacted *Jane Eyre* in passable English for a small but enthusiastic audience.

Before we left, we stopped to look at the art show. While I admired the paintings, Mrs. Kahata talked with one of the teachers, who then quietly disappeared. It was the English teacher, she told me later; he had specifically asked *not* to be introduced to me, fearing he would be put on the spot and asked to speak English.

Droves of students in school uniforms were arriving in bunches as we left, girls holding hands as they walked along. Our next stop was a coffeehouse to meet a group of students, invited by Mrs. Kahata and some of her English-speaking friends.

The first to arrive was Shoko. Because she had been sick when the entrance exam was given for Mito First High School, she was not admitted there, although it was clear from the first moment that she should have been in a top school. Though she spoke little English, Shoko immediately struck me as independent and strong-willed, two unusual characteristics in a Japanese girl. She had her own opinions on most subjects and wasn't afraid to express them. She was interested in both physics and history. She felt isolated, she said, but it didn't bother her. I hoped it really didn't, because compared to other girls I met, Shoko was definitely a misfit.

Then two girls, students from another high school, arrived with their teacher. Like Shoko, they were sixteen; all three girls were wearing their school uniforms. Through Mrs. Kahata, the teacher described their school: fourteen hundred students in one grade, only twenty of them in the "C" track, bound for the university. If they had done better on their exams, they would be going to Mito First High School. The "A" track, with seven hundred students, was for a diploma only and carried no prestige at all. The "B" track had about five hundred students, bound for junior college or technical college. The two girls with the teacher, Mrs. Kahata confided, were "B" track—unmotivated, unfocused, lacking ambition, and going to school only because their parents insisted on it.

Since this was Saturday, they had just finished a half day of classes. The three girls sipped soft drinks, the two girls who had arrived together occasionally glancing at Shoko, the loner. Unfortunately, Mrs. Kahata, who was supposed to be acting as interpreter, became so engrossed in conversation with the three girls that she forgot to translate for me. Since I had no idea what they were talking about, I watched. The two girls usually covered their mouths with their hands or with handkerchiefs, staring at Shoko surreptitiously, their faces impassive.

When the subject of school uniforms came up, Mrs. Kahata included me. They didn't mind uniforms, they said, but they'd like to have a different style. One stood up to show me: the skirt was too straight and would look better with pleats. But nobody wanted to be the one to go to the administration and say, "We want a change."

Shoko said it was the fashion now among girls to carry small, slim purses. She ignored the fad and carried a big one. "How can you carry your schoolbooks home in a small purse?" she asked the others. They replied that they didn't have to carry schoolbooks home, because there was plenty of time in school to do whatever homework was assigned. But Shoko insisted that she had things to go over when she got home, and she would continue to carry a big bag.

After a while, the two girls left the table. "Japanese girls always go to the toilet together," Shoko commented.

When they came back, the conversation became more intense; I was forgotten until finally I begged Mrs. Kahata to tell me what was going on. "Boys and sex," she said. One of the girls said that her mother had given her information, and she understood the biology of sex, but not much more than that. Shoko complained that her mother too had explained sex to her, saying "Don't do it," but without saying why she shouldn't. The two girls agreed that they would not have sex with boys because they would not be able to stand seeing their mothers' broken hearts if they became pregnant. Then one of them said that boys often put pressure on their girlfriends to have sex, and because the girls want to keep the boys, they give in to the pressure. The turn in the conversation caught me off guard, because everything I had read and heard indicated that Japanese high school students didn't date, much less become sexually involved.

Mrs. Kahata was doing her best to translate all of this for me, but the young male teacher and I remained spectators. Then Shoko turned to me and asked, "When is it all right to have sex?"

I was unprepared for the bluntness of the question. I thought she deserved a thoughtful, honest answer, but I was also aware that the Japanese view of sex is completely different from the Western view. There are none of the religious prohibitions that exist in our culture; sex has no more moral implications to the Japanese than eating or drinking—it's simply regarded as a physical function and a source of pleasure. On the other hand, there is a double standard: men can have sex with whomever they please, in or out of marriage; women traditionally have been expected to be virginal before marriage and faithful during marriage, although this is changing in Japan, as it is in the West. So what could I say to this earnest teenager who was awaiting an answer—as well as to the two girls hiding behind their hands and their handkerchiefs?

I made a pitch for friendship. I suggested that they needed to operate from a basis of respect and mutual understanding, rather than from pressure, curiosity, or romantic fantasy.

Shoko understood me, but she complained that it was almost impossible for girls to have friends who were boys. Then she told us about a boy she knew who played in the junior orchestra (she herself played violin). She was pleased about that friendship, because it was such a rare thing among young people in Japan.

The subject drifted away from sex, and the teacher came back into the conversation, talking about the amount of responsibility Japanese teachers have, staying long hours after school every day. I had read that some of the younger, more idealistic teachers stay to work with the clubs, but many of the older ones get away as soon as classes are over. He said that he tries to encourage "goodness" in his students, motivating them to behave well toward each other, rather than simply to get good grades in exams.

He complained that most students were unmotivated, even nihilistic. Suddenly he announced in English, "Craziness breaks nihilism." I hadn't the vaguest notion of what he meant by that, but it seemed a good way to end the discussion. We had been in the coffeehouse for three hours.

9

Universities: Getting In, Getting Out

Generic University

"**A**merican students take examinations to get out of school," someone once said. "Japanese take them to get in."

The amazing thing is that after all the work it takes to be admitted, Japanese universities are often referred to as "playpens," "sandboxes," or a kind of "Club Med"—four years of kicking back and recuperating from the stress of the previous twelve years. The university years are a vacation before students must buckle down to work long and hard for the rest of their lives. Students are the first to admit that you have to be incredibly lazy to flunk out of a Japanese university, although the rigid teaching methods that were the rule in junior high and high school prevail in universities as well—even the most prestigious.

Japanese universities have a bad reputation not only

among the Japanese themselves, but also among outside observers. I won't name the first university I visited, because I don't want to embarrass the people who took me there. The hour I spent with an English class ranks as the most frustrating I spent anywhere during my month in Japan. Maybe my expectations were too high. Maybe it had something to do with the school, a local college specializing in agriculture and teacher training with an enrollment of four thousand. It really wasn't a bad college, but everyone knew its students were noncompetitive; the truly ambitious ones had gone off to cities to attend larger, more prestigious universities.

Mr. Hatayama was late, an unusual event; I had found the Japanese to be compulsively punctual. Since I share the same trait, it presented no problem—I was always a little early so as not to keep them waiting. And so as not to keep *me* waiting, they would show up even earlier.

This time the situation was different. Mr. Hatayama arrived breathless and apologetic. He asked me to come to his office to get acquainted before his English class began. He unlocked the door and left his keys on the outside; then he couldn't remember what he had done with them. He had forgotten his wristwatch at home and his notes in the car. "I hate to wear watch, belt, shoes, and tie," he said.

It was a 10:30 class, but at 10:30 we were still in Mr. Hatayama's office. He had shown me his master's thesis on American author John Barth. Barth and Thomas Pynchon are two novelists whose work I find difficult, but these were Hatayama's favorites, the authors he taught to his English class. Hatayama didn't want to discuss literature, however. A thirty-three-year-old bachelor, he wanted to talk about love and life, about relationships between men and women, about men who prefer younger women and those who like them older. He told me about the woman he was in love with, a colleague at the same university. Since such a relationship was against the rules, they had to keep it a secret. She taught comparative literature; her specialty was Shakespeare. He had asked her to marry him, but she had not yet given him her answer.

"What's she like?" I asked him.

"She is more ambitious than I am. But I am more talented."

I mentioned that it was 10:30, since I had my watch and he didn't. "They would not know what to do if I came on time," he said, but ten minutes later we raced down three flights of stairs and across the campus. About forty students, most of them girls, clustered in the back of a large classroom with old-fashioned wooden two-seater desks lined up in crowded rows. Hatayama told them who I was, decided that the classroom setup was not conducive to good discussion, and announced that we would move to the student co-op.

This was a major error. The co-op was jammed with noisy students; there was no place to seat forty people. Next we trooped over to the library, where he found a small, empty room. But there were seats for only half the students; the rest leaned against the walls. It was now eleven o'clock.

Mr. Hatayama seemed genuinely excited to have an American writer in his class, an excitement that did not appear to be shared by his students, who stared at me with blank faces. His class in American literature was taught in Japanese, of course; most of the students understood no English. Nevertheless, we were going to have a discussion, he told them, just like in American college classes. But I didn't believe these students had ever had such an experience. For twelve years of primary and secondary education they had sat passively listening to lectures; their college classes were no different.

I don't know how Mr. Hatayama expected me to pull it

off, but I tried. I told them about the book I was working on and asked them to comment on my observation that Japanese society was going through many changes. No response. I tried a different angle: What changes had they observed personally? Somehow that got translated to "What changes have you personally been through?" Hatayama explained to me what he had asked them, and when there was no response—hardly a surprise at that point—he said, "The question was too personal."

The only person who seemed to be enjoying all of this was a twenty-three-year-old student who had gone to Australia a couple of years before and managed to stick it out for a year. This class seemed to be the opportunity he had been waiting for to tell his story about how he had arrived in Australia without any knowledge of English and how helpless he had felt. Life improved for him little by little, but it had been a difficult year. The skeleton of his story was passed on to me by Mr. Hatayama, whose English was good enough for our private discussions but whose talent for interpreting was limited. On and on the student talked, apparently triggered by a question I had asked.

No one else had anything to say. Mr. Hatayama tried harder. He wanted a discussion of serious subjects, he said, and, still caught up in his personal agenda, proposed to the students that they discuss the demands of love and work. Again no response. Then he resorted to a familiar Japanese technique: a show of hands. "How many think love is more important than work?" The women raised their hands. "How many think work is more important than love?" The men raised their hands.

Finally one of the male students (who, it turned out, could speak a little English) had a question for me. "What is more important to *you*, love or work?" Surprised, I set off on a rambling discourse on one of the dilemmas of American

143

society: how to "have it all," or at least achieve a balance. Since the class was made up mostly of women, I talked about the problems of women with career ambitions, mentioning that in the United States women have made great strides in educational careers. Women are frequently the principals of public schools, a situation unheard of in Japan. I wondered aloud what kinds of careers these students saw for themselves. I thought I detected some animation in the faces of the women students, but still no one spoke.

Mercifully, the hour ended. I felt tired and shaken, and Mr. Hatayama looked uncomfortable. "You're disappointed in them," he said. *Disturbed* was probably more accurate: Was this what Japanese education produced? In a couple of years these students would be starting their first jobs as teachers, doing the same thing to their pupils that was done to them: enforcing strict order, demanding exact attention to the curriculum, telling inquisitive students to keep quiet—hammering down the nail that stuck up.

Job season opened on September 12, the date university students who would graduate the following spring could begin visiting prospective employers. Until that date there was a ban on job hunting: college seniors were not supposed to seek interviews and companies were not supposed to begin scouting. Tentative employment agreements could be signed starting October 15.

This is the official line, but in reality about 40 percent of the seniors are already in the final stages of the job hunt by September, and secret employment pacts have already been made. Many of the prospective employees may have to take written employment examinations, but once that last hurdle is behind them, they are set for life. Or at least some are.

According to an article in the *Japan Times*, in 1987 Japanese firms were looking for 573,000 male college graduates, an increase of 10 percent over the previous year; the article did not mention the number of females to be hired, although it would be considerably smaller. Males could expect to get an average of 2.79 job offers; female students, 1.2 offers. Companies in nonmanufacturing businesses, such as finance and distribution, were expanding recruitment; manufacturers of precision machinery and automobiles, however, were cutting back, their exports falling because the yen was rising, thus making their cars and machines too expensive for people to buy with dollars.

In Japan, it doesn't matter much what students do with themselves for their four university years—having gotten into the university is what counts. In America, a student's field of study is important to employers. But top Japanese corporations like Sony and Mitsubishi hire future executives from top universities without paying attention either to what the students studied or to how well they studied. Their attitude seems to be, "If you've got what it takes to pass the entrance exams, then you've got what it takes to work for this company." A poll of company presidents showed that almost half had graduated from Tokyo University, called Todai. Next in prestige are Kyoto (also a national university) and the leading private colleges, Keio and Waseda. The same is true of high government officials—most are Todai graduates. But most students settle for much less.

In Japan, for twelve years (or more) students work hard, concentrating on getting into a good university that will guarantee them a good job and security for the rest of their lives. Sitting on this side of the Pacific Ocean, we imagine Japan as a nation of people who work for automobile and electronics firms. We believe all Japanese men work for huge corporations that promise them lifetime employment. But this is true for fewer than a third of Japan's workers; the other two-thirds work for small companies, run their own little businesses (there's a huge number of tiny retail shops, more than in the U.S.), or get some other kind of job.

And when we hear about "examination hell," we believe that everybody goes through it. This isn't so, although many people talk as though there is no life at all for anyone who doesn't go to college. Statistically, only about 29 percent of Japan's high school graduates go on to universities or junior colleges of some sort. Another 12 percent attend vocational training schools, while about 41 percent go to work. In the United States, well over half the high school graduates are college-bound.

Technical College, Tokyo

The professor's letters to me were slangy American English; it turned out that he had done graduate work in the United States in 1960. Because he was going to be visiting America most of the time I was in Japan, there was only one day we could arrange to meet—my last day in Japan.

For the past twenty-five years, Professor Amemiya has been teaching English at his old university in Tokyo; for the past twenty, he has been traveling three days a week to teach in a technical college in another part of the city. His students' goal there is to read scientific literature in English. The professor has developed his own teaching materials, having adapted the work of Ashley Montagu, an anthropologist who has written several books on race. He asked if I would talk to his classes at the technical college, and I agreed.

The first group was a class of fifty students majoring in precision-instrument design. He urged them to move to the front of the classroom; they did so reluctantly. Then he introduced me. "Tell them what you've seen so far in Japan," he said, reminding me to speak slowly and simply.

So I labored through my itinerary, trying to lighten it a little with anecdotes about my problems with slippers, with a description of the scene at the school with the flag and national anthem, with the confusion over *bath* and *bus*. But my talk wasn't slow enough or simple enough, and I had to stop every now and then to let Professor Amemiya translate for those who couldn't understand me—which was virtually everyone in the class.

I watched them literally fall asleep, one after the other. I stopped counting at six. (Perhaps my talk was incredibly boring, but *still*.) The experience was disconcerting, to say the least. No one—not even those who had managed to stay awake—had any questions; the professor, however, succeeded in prodding one of the more alert students to ask, "What kind of racial prejudice do you have in America? Have you observed any prejudice in Japan?"

What could I say in defense about the way the United States has treated—and continues to treat—blacks, native Americans, and other ethnic minorities? Certainly the prejudice was undeniable. But I had also heard plenty about prejudice in Japan.

"The students don't believe that prejudice exists in Japan," the professor said. "They insist they are not prejudiced."

So I told them about the Korean-born writer I had met in Japan who was not allowed to teach English—only one example of a long list of injustices he had suffered because he is Korean. I mentioned the *buraku-min*, a euphemism meaning "village people" used to refer to the eta, a people ethnically identical to the Japanese but always discriminated against as a separate caste because they had traditionally held the dirtiest, most demeaning jobs. I mentioned the strong streak of anti-Semitism in Japan, evidenced by the popularity of a rabid right-wing writer whose books were based on the idea that all the people he disapproved of—from the Rockefellers, Kennedys, and even the Pope to all American English teachers in Japan—were really power-mad Jews.

If the students had any reaction to what I said, it didn't show. The sleepers slumbered undisturbed. When the class ended after ninety minutes, the professor called them to the front of the room, a dozen or so at a time, and had them pose with me for a series of group photographs, which he took with his small camera.

I dreaded facing another bunch like the first for another hour and a half, but the second group was totally different. These were twenty-five civil engineering students, livelier than I had come to expect, fond of jokes, and not at all afraid of confrontation.

"Why are Americans so protective of whales?" asked one student. (Japan still hunts whales, and the United States is still trying to put a ban on it.)

"When are you Americans going to give up your filthy habit of wearing shoes inside your house?" one robust young man demanded, and everyone laughed.

"Probably never," I told him. Everyone laughed again. That was the last laugh for a while.

"Did you detect any anti-American sentiment in Hiroshima?" someone asked. (I had mentioned my recent visit there.)

Hiroshima was an intense emotional experience for me, as it must be for most Americans who visit the Peace Memorial Park and reflect on the terrible power unleashed on August 6, 1945, and on the people who died because of it.

Was the bombing really necessary? I wondered then—and still wonder. (It's still a hotly debated question among historians.) Three days later came Nagasaki. Wouldn't the war have ended quickly even without the killing of so many innocent people? I left feeling heavily burdened, not only that such a thing had happened once in my lifetime, but that the potential for infinitely more death and destruction still existed.

Several times in Japan when I met people my own age, who were children in the war, I asked them what they remembered about it. "The firebombings drove us out of Tokyo," a high school teacher in Utsunomiya recalled. "My mother was from this area, and we came back here to live, where it was safer. We began farming again."

Mrs. Murata was born the same year I was. "I remember that my mother had put our futon on the wooden fence to air, and my sister and I were riding on it, like a horse. My father had been gone for a long time; he was a prisoner of the Russians in Manchuria. My mother came out and told us about the terrible bomb. It was many miles from us. I remember thinking how good it felt to be in the sunshine. Soon the war was over, but we did not hear from my father for two more years. We didn't know if he was dead or alive, all that time."

But now this student was glaring at me, evidently hostile. "Don't you feel guilty," he demanded, "that you Americans did that to people?"

I had not found it necessary to be on guard with anyone in Japan—I had never been challenged the way I had been in South Africa and Northern Ireland, and the student's hostility surprised me.

"It should not have happened," I said. "But on the other hand, I remember Pearl Harbor." There were some snickers; only the professor and I could remember back that far. "I remember what the war did to my country and to my family." I could, at that moment, remember the announcement on the Philco radio in our living room: Japanese bomb-

149

ers had attacked U.S. ships in Pearl Harbor on December 7, 1941. Six months later, my father left to join what was then the Army Air Corps. Three years passed; one summer day my mother told me that a big bomb had been dropped in Japan and that my father would be home soon.

"It shouldn't have happened. Hiroshima and Nagasaki should not have happened. Pearl Harbor should not have happened. I don't feel guilty, but I do feel that it must never happen again."

After the class Professor Amemiya and I went out to eat tempura and talk about the students. I said I was surprised at their hostility, considering they were born so many years after those terrible events. I told him about people I knew whose memories had not faded: they remember what happened to their friends in Bataan in the spring of 1942, when U.S. and Filipino troops captured by the Japanese were subjected to the infamous "death march," in which thousands died. Some people remembered the time so well that even now they would not buy a Japanese car. I hadn't mentioned that in the class.

"I go often to the Philippines," the professor told me. "I visit Bataan and try to understand how *that* could have happened. It's as hard for me to comprehend as Hiroshima and Nagasaki."

At the end of the class Professor Amemiya had taken more group pictures. A week after I returned home, the prints arrived in the mail. In each one, I was the only person smiling.

10

The Dark Side

Yoyogi Park

I wanted to go to Tokyo's Yoyogi Park. I had heard that it was a hangout for rebellious teenagers, who supposedly arrive on Sunday afternoons in their school uniforms, lugging transistor radios and big shopping bags. The young rebels duck behind bushes and change into elaborate costumes they bring with them, outfits that identify them as members of a certain group. Then they turn on the radios and begin to dance in their groups—boys with boys and girls with girls. These kids with their punk outfits and their rock music were described several years ago by *Time* as part of a kind of group rebellion. Naturally I wanted to see what this rebellion was like. Maiko and Mr. Shirota agreed to meet me at the subway stop near the park at two o'clock on a Sunday.

But Yoyogi Park didn't live up to its reputation. There

151

were lots of food and soft-drink booths, and ordinary-looking people of all ages strolled in the sunshine. A few rock bands courteously set up their amps far enough apart so that the bands didn't intrude on one another's auditory space. A few menacing-looking types with hairlines shaved like samurai were dressed in black leather pants and jackets, but it was hot and they looked sweaty and miserable. Some sported pompadours. Three guys in fifties jackets and nerd sunglasses did a tap-dance routine. Athletic young daredevils raced their skateboards and jumped them over ramps. The most interesting event was a father trying to knock his daughter's purse out of a tree, but we couldn't figure out how it had gotten up there in the first place. For two hours we wandered around waiting for something rebellious to happen. Nothing did.

"That's changing," Maiko said. "Crowds of resistant teenagers used to come here, but no more."

The absence of defiant teenagers in Yoyogi Park does not, however, indicate an absence of problems among Japanese youth. In fact, the problems are increasing.

Japanese education, like Japanese society as a whole, seems to be a neat, well-ordered system in which everyone has a proper place and plays a proper role. It is a sharp contrast to American education and American society, where there is considerably more variety, more individuality—and, undeniably, where there are more problems.

Americans worry about the high drop-out rate; in Albuquerque, where I live, 20 percent of high school students quit school before they graduate. In Japan, the national average is about 6 percent. Americans worry about high illiteracy rates: about 20 percent of the U.S. population can't read simple signs or fill out basic forms, let alone read a daily newspaper. In Japan, only 2 or 3 percent of the people are illiterate. Americans worry about the poor performance of our students in math and science, and we are appalled when a study reveals that most kids can't find the United States on a map of the world. The Japanese dramatically outperform American students in such areas. As a rule, Japanese students and their parents take education seriously and make it a top priority in their lives; as a rule, Americans don't.

Americans are troubled, with good reason, about violence in schools, juvenile delinquency, and teenage suicides. Statistically, the Japanese have far less to be concerned about in these areas. But Japan's discipline and hard work have also produced a life that is highly stressful. Japanese students are subjected to an enormous amount of pressure, and the results are not always positive.

Hotline

A smiling, gray-haired woman showed up at the talk I was giving to kindergarten mothers, and at first I thought she was a visiting grandmother. But while the mothers were reticent when I begged them to ask questions, this woman had a lot on her mind: What do you do about latchkey children in the United States? What age is the proper time to begin sex education?

Later at lunch I learned that she and four other women are paid by the prefecture to operate a telephone counseling service for children. Her calls are from kids with problems and with nobody to talk to—kids whose numbers increase as more mothers go out to work. It's a busy hotline—one day she took sixty calls. The majority are fairly brief, but one caller kept her on the line for 2½ hours. Most of her callers are primary and junior high school children. "The questions often have to do with friendships," she said. "Many of the children feel terribly isolated. As the pressure increases for getting higher and higher exam scores, lots of children can't keep up, and they feel as though they're being left behind."

Suicide

Different studies yield different kinds of statistics. According to a recent survey by the Japanese Ministry of Education, the teenage suicide rate rose in 1986: 268 primary school, junior high, and senior high school students committed suicide that year—53 more than the year before. Of the 268, 14 were in primary school, 110 in junior high, and 144 in senior high school.

One set of statistics shows that the suicide rate in Japan for people ages fifteen to nineteen dropped 43 percent during the decade from 1975 through 1984, while at the same time the rate in the U.S. increased 17 percent and is now higher than Japan's. Another set of statistics indicates that although the rate for young Japanese males is dropping, the rate for girls remains high.

In 1983 *Time* reported that the suicide rate for Japan's general population was 15 per 100,000—higher than in the U.S. but lower than in most of Europe. And an article in the *Atlantic Monthly* pointed out that although the teenage suicide rate is actually lower in Japan than in the U.S., the cases seem much more flamboyant in Japan, maybe because suicide is an ancient and honorable tradition dating back to the samurai.

Apparently it is *not* true that suicide results from worry over exams or disappointment at failing to pass entrance exams to elite universities. Not liking school or not getting along in school may have more to do with adolescent suicide in Japan.

In fact, Thomas Rohlen writes in *Japan's High Schools* that as the percentage of Japanese students involved in exam wars goes up, the suicide rate for that age group goes down. He believes that youth suicide is a bigger problem among those who do poorly in school, can't keep up academically, and tend to drop out early. Those who drop out can get only low-paying jobs without any security and are destined to a life at the bottom of society. The pressure is greater on them than on those who stick it out through "examination hell."

Juvenile Delinquency

Compared to the United States, Japan has a minor problem with juvenile delinquency. Yet the problem is growing, and everyone worries about it. In 1979 arrests of youthful offenders jumped by 48 percent.

There are several reasons why Japan has relatively little delinquency. Japanese society is homogeneous, without frictions between minority groups. It is highly structured and highly disciplined. And Japanese young people are closely supervised—they're either at home, at school, or going from one to the other. Many students spend at least an hour a day riding trains or buses to school or pedaling three-speed bicycles.

High school students are not permitted to try out adult fashions or activities. They dress conservatively, even out of school. They're not allowed to drive cars until they are eighteen, although sixteen-year-olds can get a license to drive motorbikes if their schools permit them (most don't). And teenagers generally are not sexually involved. The Japanese are conscious of what's proper and what is not, and falling in love or engaging in sex in one's teens definitely comes under the heading of "not proper."

When teenagers do rebel, it is often in the form of altering their school uniform, perming their hair, or smoking. Cigarette smoking is forbidden in high schools, and teenagers caught smoking on the streets are hauled off to the police station. Repeat offenses can mean expulsion from school. Few young people drink; some sniff glue. There are practically no drugs: marijuana and hard drugs are virtually unavailable in Japan, although use of speed, brought in from Taiwan and Korea, is on the rise.

Schools are involved in the lives of students even when students are away from school grounds; rules cover curfews, dress codes, and such forbidden territory as coffee shops, pachinko parlors, and other places deemed undesirable. Parents enforce school rules, sometimes patrolling the neighborhood to make sure the rules are being obeyed.

School and police work together; both the school disciplinary counselor and the parents must appear at the police station when a student gets into trouble. The conviction rate in Japan is high—99 percent of those who are actually brought to trial—but hardly any students actually go to jail. Instead they are placed under the supervision of volunteer parole workers called *hogoshi*.

One day I talked with the probation officer in Tochigiken, who works for the Ministry of Justice. He told me about *hogoshi*, who usually deal with theft problems of various kinds—teenagers who steal bicycles and motorcycles, shoplift, and commit other relatively minor crimes. *Hogoshi* are chosen as model citizens, people who are stable both economically and personally and have a reputation for kindness and generosity. Because younger people who fulfill all these criteria usually don't have much free time to spend with youthful offenders, most *hogoshi* are retired people. That creates a significant generation gap, but because of the traditional veneration for the elderly, the gap isn't a serious problem. There are several thousand *hogoshi* throughout Japan, about eight hundred of them in Tochigi-ken.

Ijime: *Bullying*

Five or ten years ago, the probation officer said, the main problem was school violence in the form of attacks against teachers. Violence was particularly prevalent in junior high schools, where pupils sometimes pulled knives on teachers. But now the violence has turned against other kids. Bullying—or *ijime*, as it's called—is the major problem, especially in junior high schools. Someone is singled out who seems somehow different, who doesn't fit in, who may be weak or doing poorly in school, and that person is tormented by the group. *Ijime* takes the form of teasing and ostracism as well as physical violence and can result in both physical and psychological damage to the victim. Bullying is a particularly powerful Japanese phenomenon, and it works terrifyingly well because Japan is so group-oriented. The need to fit in, the need not to stand out, makes life unbearable for someone being subjected to *ijime*.

According to a newspaper report, 52,600 cases of bullying were reported in 1986, down by a third from the 1985 level. But in 1985 twelve suicides were attributed to *ijime*, and sixty junior high school students were arrested. The story is told of a thirteen-year-old who was bullied mercilessly; classmates at his junior high even held a mock funeral for him, attended by fifty students and four teachers. The boy hanged himself.

According to the probation officer, a lot of kids hate

157

school. Rigid methods of instruction and intense pressure are two reasons; *ijime* is a third. Thus, it grows harder and harder to keep kids in school.

Everybody blames somebody else for this situation. The probation officer blames the teachers, many of whom are poorly trained. They may know their subject matter, he says, but they don't know pedagogical techniques or developmental psychology. Many teachers don't really like kids, and they haven't the faintest notion of how to deal with them. The kids resent it, become frustrated, and turn their anger against someone else. It used to be the teachers themselves who felt the brunt of that anger. During the time of the most school violence, it was not the old, experienced teachers who were attacked, but the young ones.

Right-wing critics of the educational system blame the postwar decline in traditional values, laying the responsibility on the American occupation and the influence of democracy. Their solution is to make already rigid school rules even more rigid. But the left-wing Japan Teachers' Union, Nikkyoso, blames authoritarianism and the pressure of the examination system.

Taibatsu

Alex Shishin, an American teacher, is an outspoken critic of Japanese education. Married to a Japanese high school teacher, Shishin himself is an assistant professor at Miyazaki Women's Junior College. With over eight years' teaching experience in Japan, he writes frequently about educational issues. I came across some of his articles in an English-language magazine, and tried to contact him when I got to Miyazaki. Somehow we always missed each other, but within days after I returned home, a thick envelope arrived from him with photocopies of his various articles. One was on a subject I had not heard mentioned in Japan: *taibatsu*, corporal punishment in the schools.

It's illegal for a teacher to strike a student, but teachers will be fired for inflicting such punishment only if it results in death or serious injury. If enough parents complain, teachers who hit students may be reprimanded, but, according to Shishin, *taibatsu* is popular among military-minded educators. *Taibatsu* can range from a slap on the behind to something as sadistic as sticking pins in the stomach of girl students—supposedly to teach them safety.

Shishin calls *taibatsu* "Japanese education's open dirty secret." He quotes a survey of freshmen at a prefectural university, a survey revealing that "each student polled was punished physically an average of twenty-three times [during junior and senior high], 26 percent of the students suffering injuries." When Shishin reviewed *Japanese Education Today*, the report written by the U.S. Department of Education, he praised it, saying it was "better than many current books about Japanese schooling." He also criticized it, however—not only for failing to mention the use of physical and mental cruelty in Japanese schools but, in fact, for stating just the opposite: that school violence "rarely includes teacher violence against students."

Shishin thinks there is an "industry" promoting a false favorable picture of Japanese education. He paints a vastly different portrait. "The Japanese educational system is fundamentally bad," he writes, "though on the surface it may look like a behaviorist's paradise. . . . It is outdated, mind-destroying, and antidemocratic. The Japanese educational system's best lesson for America is: Don't let this happen to you."

Part Three

JAPANESE FAMILIES: THE INNER CIRCLE

11

Olδ Traδitions,
Changing Times

Kahata Family

D r. Kahata is a cardiovascular surgeon, a
tall, good-humored man who works for
a government hospital. "That means we're not rich," his
wife explained. Dr. Kahata's English is fair, but not up to
detailed explanations of the economics of medicine in Japan;
Mrs. Kahata's is entirely adequate.

"If he were in private practice, he would make a lot more
money," she said. "In Japan, all doctors are paid the same
salary, no matter how much training they've had in spe-
cialties like cardiovascular surgery. Everybody starts out the
first year working for a hospital at the same salary level.
Then you get increases according to seniority. It has nothing
to do with merit or training."

"You go into private practice if you want to make money,"
Dr. Kahata said. "You open your own hospital."

Mrs. Kahata fixed dinner while we talked in the kitchen of their home in Mito, a city of two hundred thousand located an hour away by train from Tokyo. I had been invited to stay there for one night. Most of what I learned about the Japanese, I learned in their homes. Although I was an outsider, I had the rare privilege of staying with several Japanese families and participating, if only briefly and superficially, in their lives. Even from such short exposure, it was evident that some families were rather traditional, while others were not; but all were experiencing changes.

The doctor's house was large by Japanese standards. In traditional Japanese families, the young married couple moves in with the husband's parents. But in this case, his parents wanted a place to themselves. The elder Mrs. Kahata is now hospitalized from an "attack of the brain," and the old man lives alone in a little house separated from the main house by a small yard. A mongrel dog snoozed in a doghouse in one corner of the yard. Laundry flapped on a compact clothesline.

The three Kahata children wandered in and out. The twelve-year-old son was watching television in the next room. His ten-year-old sister and seven-year-old brother knelt at a low table and folded paper to make origami figures. Children learn to make paper cranes in kindergarten, and I asked them to show me how to do it. They worked with me patiently on each complicated fold until I finally managed. The two younger Kahata children take piano lessons, practicing about a half hour a day. The older boy, Mrs. Kahata confided, is not interested in piano, origami or sports or much of anything. She worries about him, about his lack of focus. The two younger children are always busy, always involved, but the oldest one—nothing. At this point, ready to begin junior high school in a few months, he should be focused on his schoolwork, thinking about his future.

Mrs. Kahata apologized a couple of times for her casualness, but it needed no apology. We talked while she breaded pork cutlets and fried them, mixed potato salad, broiled little fish on a rack, and dished up rice from the electric rice cooker, a standard appliance in Japanese homes. When the meal was ready, the children came to the table, ate quickly without much conversation, and left. We three adults lingered at the table over coffee.

They told me how they had met. "Ours was an arranged marriage," she said. "Our fathers were university students together. They remained friends. One had a thirty-two-year-old son who was an established surgeon and needed a wife. The other had a twenty-five-year-old daughter. My two younger sisters were urging me to get married and get out of the house. They worried that after twenty-five, my chances of finding a husband were dwindling! So our two fathers, both doctors, decided to introduce us."

Arranged marriages are still common in Japan. At one time they were the rule; now they account for about half the marriages. They are arranged with the consent of both people. A man and woman are introduced by a friend of the families or a hired third party. If they like each other they proceed, but if they don't, they are under no obligation to marry or to see each other again. In the old days, marriages were often arranged for political or economic reasons; today the old custom simply seems to be a good way to get people from similar backgrounds together, people who might have much in common.

The doctor and his bride-to-be met once and decided on the spot that it was a good match. That was in October; six months later they were married. They saw each other only two or three times in between. They didn't think it was necessary to get acquainted; they would have the rest of their lives to do that.

"When I first met him I thought, this will be all right,"

she said. "I'm not a perfectionist. I'm not very good at cooking and cleaning and keeping everything orderly. I don't like to bother with fashion. I thought he wouldn't mind any of that. But most important, I liked his mother, and I thought that if I liked the mother, then the son was bound to be all right too."

His impression of her—he spoke in Japanese and she translated—was that she was nice and didn't wear a lot of makeup; he didn't like "painted women." She described family backgrounds that were virtually identical, and the two similar temperaments. The Kahatas seemed to have a solid marriage, but probably not an exciting one. Excitement, though, isn't what Japanese marriages are about. The main goal is having children, and the children become the primary focus. Western—particularly *American*—ideas of romance and companionship in marriage seem irrelevant to most Japanese.

Mrs. Kahata described herself as a "good Japanese wife," which to her means staying at home to take care of the house and children. A survey comparing the attitudes of Chinese and Japanese women concluded that the Chinese are more liberated: the Japanese believe more strongly that the woman's role is to be the homemaker and the man must be the breadwinner. But the fact is that many mothers do go out to work, some from choice, more from economic necessity.

Mrs. Kahata says that if she decided to get a job, it would disrupt their lives. "I don't want very much," she said. "We don't need the extra income to buy luxuries. My luxury is having free time to study French, to read, to listen to music and play the piano, and to be with my children."

I was given an upstairs room with a futon, some quilts, and a pillow. There seemed to be other rooms upstairs; the doors were closed when I arrived, but the next morning a couple of the doors were open to a large mat room, containing three futons lined up next to each other, a single futon placed a little apart. Mrs. Kahata slept there with the children, she said. Dr. Kahata? I didn't ask.

Having the whole family sleep together in one room is common in Japan, although when children reach high school age they are usually given a room of their own so they can study. It's not unusual for the husband to sleep in another room. According to some sources, after the children are born sex is no longer of much importance for Japanese couples. As mentioned earlier, there are no religious or moral taboos against sex in Japan: men are free to find sexual pleasure outside of marriage, but wives are expected to remain faithful to their husbands. Homosexuality is acceptable. In many Japanese families, the wife's most intimate contact is with her children—particularly with her sons.

Because Dr. and Mrs. Kahata enjoyed music, I asked if she and her husband liked going to concerts. "No," she said, "we have not gone out together since our oldest son was born. It would not be appropriate for me to have someone come in to take care of the children." Recently there had been a concert in Mito, and her husband had asked her to go with him. "Of course I told him I couldn't," she said. "My responsibility is to be with my children." He went alone and told her later that there had been other couples at the concert. She was pleased, she said, that he wanted her to go with him. "Maybe in the future I will consider it," she conceded, but as long as the children were at home, she probably would not. (Since her youngest was only seven, her husband would have a long time to wait.)

"Women are judged totally on how their children turn out," she said. "Everyone is afraid to take the chance of doing something for herself that might somehow be bad for the children."

We spent Saturday morning at the Mito First High School festival and Saturday afternoon with a group of high school girls in a coffee shop, Mrs. Kahata acting as interpreter. It was a long day, and at five o'clock, she announced that she had to get home. That night I stayed with another family, but Mrs. Kahata picked me up early Sunday morning to catch a train. On the way to the station, she told me about the situation she had found when she arrived home the day before. Her husband was there when the children came in at one o'clock from a half day of school, but when Mrs. Kahata had not yet returned by three, her daughter began to get upset. When she finally got home shortly after five, the ten-year-old girl was weeping inconsolably, convinced that her mother had gone off with the *gaijin*.

"Do you think I've spoiled my children?" she asked me.

Not in the sense of indulging them, I said, but I thought they seemed very dependent on her. "But that's what I wanted!" she exclaimed. "I'm glad they need me so much!"

Many experts have written about the dependency of Japanese children on their mothers. Some say this carries over into the employee's dependency on the company he works for. Many young men have trouble breaking away from their mothers even after they marry. They often put unrealistic expectations on their wives, discovering soon after the wedding that the young bride is not going to take perfect care of him as his mother always did.

Itagaki Family

The house was large and luxurious; it was reached through a narrow alley off a commercial street within sight and earshot of the railroad. A smiling woman met me at the door with her two sons, one home from Waseda University in Tokyo where he studies physics, the other a fifteen-year-old high school student in Utsunomiya.

I left my shoes by the door, slid into slippers set out for me, and followed the younger son up the stairs to my room. But the stairs had open risers, nothing to stop the slipper as it shot off my foot down into the hall below. My slipper problems amused the family. The boy set my bags in a large mat room and showed me the Western-style room next to it that I could use as an office if I wished. Across the hall was a parlor with a magnificent Yamaha grand piano, kept under lock and key. Downstairs they ushered me into the living room with *tatami*, a table, pillows, and floor chairs.

Later on I figured out that this wasn't their house. It belonged to Mrs. Itagaki's father-in-law, the owner of a small manufacturing company. Her husband works for his father, and they live in a much smaller house next door to the factory. They pointed it out to me when we stopped by the factory, but I was not invited inside. Most Japanese never entertain guests at home because their houses are so small and crowded. Mrs. Itagaki, a friend of Mrs. Murata, had arranged for me to stay at the home of the grandparents, who were away for the weekend.

At six on a Saturday evening Mrs. Itagaki's husband was still in his office; the other workers had just left, except for the man sweeping up. The factory visit was the only time I met Mr. Itagaki: like most Japanese men, he worked long hours. (It was also possible that he didn't want to be involved with entertaining *gaijin*.)

Although Japanese society is male-dominated, the Japanese family operates differently. The wife may work hard nurturing her husband's fragile ego, but it is she who controls the purse strings and determines how the family income is to be spent. The husband hands over his paycheck, and the wife gives him an allowance. She's the one who does the family budgeting, decides what to buy, and directs the children's education, although at home she waits on him and in public may walk slightly behind him. At one time it was the husband's mother who held the real power in the family. That's changing, but has not disappeared.

Mrs. Itagaki and her sons treated me like a visiting head of state. There was little of the informality I had enjoyed sitting in Mrs. Kahata's kitchen and watching her make potato salad. They took me out for dinner and insisted that I eat steak, a luxury in Japan. They fixed bacon and eggs for breakfast ("You like sunny up?" asked the younger boy, who was studying English conversation but hadn't quite gotten the hang of it), since that's what Americans expect for breakfast. The older brother, who works part-time as an international telephone operator and speaks good English, entertained me with anecdotes about his job.

They took me to a *kendo* class, *kendo* being a form of Japanese fencing, where for a couple of hours I watched well-padded, steel-visored kids whack the daylights out of each other with bamboo swords. They drove me to a couple of high school festivals, and they found a calligrapher who would give me a demonstration of his craft. They spent hours preparing an elaborate sushi meal, the younger son patiently fanning the rice in a wooden tub to remove the moisture. In the evening, they played Mozart on the grand piano. And when it was arranged for me to go to Nikko, Mrs. Itagaki's younger brother, Mr. Akutsu, was assigned as chauffeur.

Mr. Akutsu had been drafted to drive me to a resort area famous for its beautiful scenery as well as its shrines and temples, leave me there overnight at a youth hostel, and pick me up at noon the next day to take me back to Utsunomiya. I tried to assure Mr. Akutsu that I could take a bus or a train, but he was insistent, and I finally concluded that he must be looking forward to having some time off.

Little by little his story came out. Akutsu's field is computers, and for ten years he worked in Tokyo for one of the big newspapers. But when his mother's health began to fail, he returned from Tokyo to be with her and went to work for his sister's father-in-law. He doesn't particularly like this job, and would rather be back in Tokyo.

Akutsu was past thirty when his mother died, and he decided it was time to marry. He employed the services of a professional matchmaker, who brought him the photograph of a young woman and a description of what she was like—her character and background, her interests. The woman also got a description of him. They went out for a meal together and liked each other. For the next several months they saw each other regularly and got acquainted. And then, since neither of them had backed out of the arrangement, they planned a marriage.

Akutsu wanted a small wedding, but his bride wanted a big one—so they had a large, expensive wedding at a wedding hall. He wanted to go to Hokkaido for a honeymoon, but his bride wanted Hawaii—so they flew to Hawaii. "I went completely crazy there spending money," he said. "A coral necklace for my sister, all kinds of expensive gifts for everybody. We spent thousands of dollars."

That was five years ago. His wife is a school nurse who makes more money than he does, and he admits he has mixed feelings about that. She wants a baby badly, but so far they have not had one, and she cries when she sees babies on television. He is not so anxious to be a father, he says.

Dutiful son, dutiful husband, dutiful brother who volunteered to drive the American visitor. Duty is an important concept to the Japanese; it governs most of their relation-ships. In *The Chrysanthemum and the Sword,* her landmark book about the Japanese written in 1946, American anthro-pologist Ruth Benedict describes the complex obligations and indebtedness that Japanese are bound to honor—that are more important than the wishes and desires of the individual.

I had read a news item about a brother and sister who were involved in a hit-and-run incident resulting in the death of a teenage boy. The sister turned herself in a few hours later, but it eventually came out that it was the brother who was behind the wheel. Afraid that her brother, the sole support of their aged parents, would be imprisoned, the girl tried to take his place. But when the truth emerged, the brother hanged himself. I mentioned the news item to Mrs. Murata. "It is a very Japanese story," she said, "a story of duty and dishonor."

Whenever I talked with Japanese writers about their books, we pondered why their work had not been translated into English. One suggestion was that the conflicts are quite different: Americans like happy endings with a heavy dose of romance, while Japanese traditionally are caught up in themes of obligation and honor. We had all seen *The Grad-uate,* a film made in the sixties, and remembered the won-derful ending in which Dustin Hoffman seizes Kathryn Ross in her wedding gown and runs away with her in a bus. When I saw the movie years ago, the audience cheered.

"In Japan," one writer said, "it would be the story of the bridegroom left standing at the altar." "The two would never have married," someone else suggested. "They might have made a suicide pact and jumped off a cliff together."

One night I watched a TV movie that seemed like a Jap-anese remake of *The Graduate.* I couldn't understand the dialogue, of course, but I could generally follow the action, which cut back and forth between a young man in a great hurry to get somewhere and a bride on her way to her wedding. One thing after another happened to the poor fellow—his car ran out of gas, he commandeered a truck— while the bride marched unhappily down the aisle toward the groom. Just as the truck screeched to a halt outside, the bride stopped in the midst of her vows, turned, and fled from the church. The young man leapt from the truck, embraced the bride, and the two drove off together, pursued in a helicopter by the startled groom and shocked father of the bride.

If duty and obligation traditionally win out over romantic happy endings in Japanese fiction, that too is changing.

Yoshida Family

Mrs. Yoshida looks like a Japanese doll. Her dark hair swings straight and shining just above her shoulders, blunt-cut with thick, straight bangs. She apologized for treating me so informally and promised that when I came again it would be different. But I liked it this way. The pressure was off both of us.

Her husband, a scientist employed by the government, was in Canada for a few weeks. Because of space problems, I probably would not have been invited if he had been at home. Their home is small, cramped for a family of five— a duplex apartment in one of the dreary blocks of concrete buildings owned by the government and rented to government employees at a comparatively low cost. It reminded me of dreary low-income government housing in the U.S., serviceable, but dingy.

We took the elevator to the fifth floor and walked along an outside balcony, making our way among toys and tricycles. The door opened into a tiny entryway littered with shoes, not with the toes all neatly pointed out, as I had been taught, but tumbled every which way. The one large room on the first floor had a tiny kitchen tucked into one corner and Western-style furniture—a large dining table and chairs, a china cabinet filled with family treasures, a sectional sofa, and a television set with a VCR on which the three-year-old endlessly played and replayed *Mary Poppins*. Near the front door was the washstand; outside, a very small toilet. A calendar hung on the toilet-room wall, with a new English word to learn every day. The calendar was turned to February 4, 1984; the word for the day was *rhombus*. Next to the calendar hung a key chain with hundreds of cards, Japanese on one side, English on the other: *exercise, expedition*. . . . Mrs. Yoshida had studied English in an unusual college that taught by "direct method," using English-only classrooms, and she had spent a few months in the United States. Conversation was easy.

The bathroom was on the second floor of the apartment, along with three small mat rooms and a crowded hall with a little washing machine. One room seemed to be used for "stuff;" a second room, where I slept on a futon, was lined with bookshelves and had a desk and chair; the third was furnished with a set of bunk beds for the two older children. Mrs. Yoshida and her husband slept on the floor on futons; the baby had her own small mat next to theirs. "That's the way we do it in Japan," she said. "When my son is a little older, he'll get his own room, and the baby will sleep in the bunk."

It was from Mrs. Yoshida that I learned about child rearing in Japan. When her first child was born, it was delivered by Caesarian section. She had chosen the hospital for the birth because it was near her parents' home (since it was expected that her mother would help her afterwards), but it was a hospital with old-fashioned policies. Since Mrs. Yoshida was a surgical patient, she was kept in the surgical ward, and her newborn son was taken off to the nursery in the maternity ward. For five days she was kept in bed and not allowed to see her baby. Everyone else had seen him, of course. "The family is more important than the individual in Japan," she said. "My son instantly became the property of the Yoshida family, and my feelings were not considered."

I saw a copy of Dr. Spock's *Baby and Child Care* on one of her shelves; that had been the "bible" when my own children were small, and many Japanese mothers still follow his advice. "But often the Japanese way wins out," she said, explaining that she and her friends breastfed their babies every three hours. She seemed to be nursing the baby more or less constantly. "My mother thinks I'm crazy," she said.

Mrs. Yoshida doesn't carry the baby on her back, as mothers used to, but astride her hip. The baby, a cheerful little girl who rarely cried, smiled contentedly as long as she was around people. Mrs. Yoshida stayed with the baby when she put her down for a nap, singing to her quietly until she dropped off to sleep. But the three-year-old girl bounced on the furniture and interrupted conversation, demanding attention and getting it. The nine-year-old son, on the other hand, remained aloof.

It was also from Mrs. Yoshida and her friends that I learned about marriage Japanese-style. Mrs. Yoshida invited some women for morning tea, thinking I would be interested in their experiences living abroad. Like Mrs. Yoshida, they were university graduates, married to scientists whose work often took them overseas. Yet in many ways these women were traditional in their outlook.

Mrs. Yoshida talked about the college she had attended, a women's college founded by Western missionaries who encouraged students to develop their potential. The girls took the advice to heart, but were now paying the price. "Half the women in my class are divorced," she said.

The divorce rate in Japan is only about a quarter of what it is in the United States, but it's increasing rapidly. Since women are generally discriminated against in the work force, and since they have little experience and can't get jobs that pay them well, most divorced women go home to live with their parents. "It's a terrible situation," she said. "There is no outlet for their talents—but there wasn't when they were married, either. Good jobs for women are scarce. While they were married, they focused totally on their children. But now they're back with their parents, completely dependent on them, living like children themselves."

Some high-achieving Japanese women have formed a network, inviting only women who have become successful on their own. There are about fifty members in this elite group; the average age is forty-seven, and half are either divorced or single. Some of the divorcées claimed their husbands had left because they felt their wives weren't taking good enough care of them, and they wanted to find someone who would.

Women now have a certain amount of economic independence, although statistically they earn about 60 percent of what men are paid. "They have emotional independence," Mrs. Kakegawa, the translator, had told me. "Many women are discovering that they don't need men as much as they thought they did. This is very frightening to men, who sometimes leave the wife because they're afraid that if they don't leave first, their wives will leave them."

"Is it true," Mrs. Yoshida's friends asked, "that American husbands help with the children?"

One of Mrs. Yoshida's friends was married to a man now working in the Philippines. She had brought the children back to Japan when her oldest son was in junior high school, but her husband would be gone for another year. "Do you miss him?" Mrs. Yoshida asked. The woman laughed.

According to one Japanese proverb, "a good husband is healthy and absent." The wife's primary relationship is with her children, these women told me. "A husband and wife who appear to have a romantic relationship and who put themselves first are seen to be immature," Mrs. Yoshida said. "Women make their own lives and have their own friends."

"What do women look for in a husband?" I asked them.

"*Not* the oldest son," one replied, and they all agreed. If you married the oldest son, you were expected to live with your in-laws and take responsibility for them in their old age. Though these women claimed that the mother-in-law, once all-powerful in Japan, had lost much of her power, I talked to others who disagreed. The mother-in-law was more manipulative now, some maintained, since she couldn't call the shots outright.

Mrs. Yoshida mentioned a recent survey asking women what they wanted in a man; most respondents had listed "bravery" and "tenderness." "But," another had said, "when women do find a man they think is gentle, they usually believe he is weak."

Japanese women cultivate passivity, or at least the appearance of it. Girls learn that role when they're very young. Boys are brought up to believe in masculine superiority; girls find out early that they are less important than their brothers. They learn to present two faces, the private and the public. Like most Americans, I think, I prefer people who are what they seem to be. But in Japan the "iron fist in the velvet glove" is the model. "Like the women in *Gone with the Wind*," one of Mrs. Yoshida's friends suggested.

In the elevator Mrs. Yoshida introduced me to a woman carrying an infant and leading a toddler and a school-age child. Later she explained that the woman had studied to be a pastry chef in France and now taught fancy baking classes. "She's very strong, very independent," Mrs. Yoshida said; "but you'd never know it. She plays the game of being passive and accepting."

Miss Mishima, who lives in Mito, speaks English almost perfectly, with an accent so good that at first I thought she might be American-born. That talent allows her to command a top salary; she teaches at four different colleges. An only child, she lives with her widowed mother. She recently bought herself a new car and learned to drive. She enjoys her money and her independence, but her mother disapproves of her ambitious goals.

"Goals aren't usually expressed in Japan," Miss Mishima said. "It's considered bad form to show that you are ambitious, particularly if you're a girl." She described a seminar she had once attended, where college women talked about their goals—cautiously, being careful to understate them. She had told the other women that she wanted to go to graduate school—a low-risk statement, since even though getting into graduate school was a competitive business, Miss Mishima was certain she'd be accepted somewhere. But she had been careful not to state which graduate school she wanted to attend, particularly the prestigious one she had in mind.

One of the other women had not been so reticent. She'd announced that she wanted to be a politician, because she wanted to change Japan! Everyone was shocked at such a statement, and immediately they turned against her.

"What happened to her?" I asked.

"She went to America and became a journalist," Miss Mishima said.

178

Mrs. Koyama

Mrs. Koyama's mother-in-law babysat for her so she could take me sightseeing in Kyoto. Mrs. Koyama was free every day but Tuesday, the day she took her class in patchwork quilting, Japan's newest rage. Women who used to study tea ceremony or flower arranging now learn to piece bits of fabric together to make American-looking quilts.

Not much of a sightseer, I chose instead to wander through some of the old neighborhoods while we talked. All of my descriptions of Japanese women sound much the same because Japanese women look much the same to Westerners—small, slender, fine-boned, dark-haired, variations occurring mostly in hairstyle. Mrs. Koyama fit the description; her hair was cut short. After she graduated from college, where she studied English, she taught for a while and then got a job at a travel agency—and married her boss. Now they have two sons, one in elementary school, the other about to start nursery school in the spring.

Her husband is an oldest son, she told me; therefore, they live with his parents. I told her about the women who had warned "Don't marry the oldest son!"

"They're right," she said. "It means a lot of responsibility. The oldest son must take care of his parents and support them financially in their old age. The mother often dominates her son and makes her daughter-in-law miserable."

"Is that the way it is with your family?"

"No," she said. "My mother-in-law is very nice, sweet and gentle and easy to get along with. My husband has always encouraged me to do what I want to do. But my father-in-law is difficult. And my husband's younger brother lives with us, too. He has never married. So I have to look after all these people and cook three sets of meals—one for the old people, one for the children, and one for us. Fortunately I like to cook."

179

Mr. and Mrs. Koizumi

Mrs. Koizumi, her silvery hair combed in soft waves, invited me to meet her and her husband at a French restaurant. An elderly gentleman seated at the head of the table, he responded to the introduction, but soon his attention drifted away. He was a graduate of Todai and taught English for many years. His graduate studies were on Ralph Waldo Emerson, nineteenth-century American essayist and poet.

When he retired from teaching, Mr. Koizumi bought an office building in Mito, leased most of the space to a bank, and managed an art gallery on the top floor and a coffeehouse on the lower level. Then came a series of strokes and loss of memory. Now he forgets who he is and where he is; his wife puts tags on him so that if he wanders away, someone will find him and call her to come get him. But he takes the tags off and sometimes disappears for hours at a time. Mrs. Koizumi has taken over managing the art gallery and the coffeehouse—this in addition to directing a private kindergarten. "I become exhausted," she said. "But it is good that I have much to do. It keeps my mind off my life." She didn't mention her children.

I handed Mr. Koizumi my demonstration copy of *Voices of South Africa*. He took it with interest and turned to the first page, but in seconds his attention wandered. The other guests arrived and the waitress began to bring the food, serving it Japanese-style, putting everything on the table at once—soup bowls, salad plates, dinner plates with the main course, all crowded together. Mr. Koizumi stared uncomprehendingly at the food. His wife helped him eat.

Japan, like other industrial nations, no longer knows how to deal with its aging population. Life expectancy in Japan is the longest in the world: eighty for women, more than seventy-four for men. But the family structure is changing, shifting from an extended family with several generations living under one roof to the nuclear family of parents and children, leaving open the question of where and how the elderly will live. Young women go out to work now, and nobody wants to marry the oldest son and take on the responsibility for his parents.

"FLIGHT OF MADAME BUTTERFLY" read the newspaper column headline. Madame Butterfly is the lead character in an opera written in 1904 by Italian composer Giacomo Puccini. A geisha who falls in love with an American naval officer, Butterfly bears him a child and then kills herself when she discovers that her "husband" already has an American wife.

Madame Butterfly symbolizes the passive Japanese woman who exists solely to cater to the needs of the male. The author of the newspaper column was examining the plight of middle-class Japanese women initially attracted to men because of the universities they attended and their career prospects—women who found too late that the men they had married were egocentric clods. Older women in Japan were raised to respect men, to defer to masculine pride and authority; they were taught to obey their husbands and endure without complaint. But younger women don't subscribe to that philosophy. Many are walking out of their lifeless marriages and getting divorces.

I mentioned this column to a woman who had been telling me about her own arranged marriage and asked if she saw any differences between arranged marriages and the non-arranged marriages typical of the West. "Whether marriages are arranged or not," she said, "Japanese women look for the wrong things in a husband: they want a man who has gone to the right schools and has the right job, so he'll be a good provider. Then they're disappointed when he turns out to be a workaholic totally centered on his job and not much interested in her."

"What's he looking for?"

"Someone pretty who comes from a good family and will look after him the way his mother has. Both of them are disappointed."

Kawahara Family

Mr. Kawahara is a rising star in the education bureaucracy. A graduate of Todai, he taught Japanese for a while at Utsunomiya Girls' High School, but now works for the prefectural board of education. Through his connections I was able to visit a number of schools. And he invited me to be his houseguest for a night.

On the evening I was to visit Mr. Kawahara and his wife, I met him at his office around six o'clock. Usually, he told me, he stayed in the office until ten or so and had to be back at work the next morning by half past eight. But that day the superintendent had given him permission to leave early to entertain the foreign visitor. The next day was a national holiday and his office was officially closed; he didn't have to go in until noon.

It was a twenty-minute bus ride to the outskirts of town and a five-minute walk past vegetable gardens to the home he himself had designed. Mr. Kawahara's wife was a pretty woman who spoke little English, a kindergarten teacher who had also worked as a fashion model. They had gone to great pains to make sure that everything was perfect. There were fresh flowers in each room—roses in the mat room where we ate, even a bouquet in the toilet room. When I commented on their beauty, he said, "That is for the guest. Normally we don't have it."

The room where I slept was equipped with a small refrigerator stocked with beer and fruit juices. As soon as her husband and I arrived, Mrs. Kawahara served green tea at the low table in the center of the room, accompanied by sweets made of bean paste and candied chestnuts. One of the wonderful touches in Japan is the steaming washcloth handed to each guest in restaurants, and often to guests in private homes. When the weather is hot, as it was then, the washcloths are sometimes chilled. Mrs. Kawahara kept some in the little refrigerator.

After the welcoming tea, Mr. Kawahara gave me a tour of his house. When ground was broken for its construction a few years before, he had hired a Shinto priest to sprinkle salt all over the ground as purification and to build a small bamboo hut in which to say prayers for the house. Someday his parents would come to live with them; his mother, now seventy, was an artist, and he had built a studio for her and equipped it with finely made wooden drawers for her watercolors and inks and slots to hold her paper and canvases. One of the beauties of Japanese architectural design is that the rooms are all basically the same: *tatami*, a low table and flat cushions in the center, closets for bedding and whatever else needs to be stashed away, an alcove to display art objects or flowers. All of this can be rearranged in a moment; a dining room becomes a bedroom in less than five minutes.

Mrs. Kawahara wasn't around much. She spent most of her time in the kitchen, bringing beer and sake and serving course after course to her husband and me. Mr. Kawahara explained each dish: a tiny hard-boiled quail egg floating in miso, bamboo shoots, tempura, a delicate custard with tofu and snow peas. After dinner we had coffee and dessert in the upstairs study. The next morning, Mrs. Kawahara served a Japanese-style breakfast—grilled smoked fish, *miso*, rice, *nori* (strips of seaweed manipulated with chopsticks around a mouthful of rice), and *natto*. Most Americans don't like it, they told me; I was no exception.

Nobuko, a college freshman, lives an hour by bus from Utsunomiya. Until this year she was a boarding student at Utsunomiya Girls' High School. Now she commutes every day from her home to her classes in Tokyo—more than two hours each way. She used her day off to come visit her former high school teacher and to meet me. We spent a couple of hours in the upstairs study not long after breakfast, drinking coffee and eating apple pie.

Nobuko, lively and forthright, described her "resistance" as a young teenager. "When I was fourteen, I fought with my mother constantly," she said. "I always wanted to be going out and seeing my friends, and she wanted me to stay at home. Now we get along very well. We don't argue at all any more. But I still like to go out a lot."

Then we were ushered into the dining area next to the kitchen for lunch. At that moment both Mr. and Mrs. Kawahara happened to be out of the room.

"Why do you think they don't have any children?" Nobuko whispered to me.

"I haven't any idea," I said.

"They've been married for several years," she said. "They've got a big house. Why don't you ask them?" she persisted.

"Because it's none of my business," I whispered. "I got into trouble at your old high school for asking where the girls wanted to go to college. I'm certainly not going to ask people why they don't have children. Why don't *you* ask them?"

"I have. Several times."

"And?"

"He won't answer. He changes the subject."

There was nothing passive and reticent about this young woman. Every now and then I met one like her, who seemed to break all the rules and didn't seem to care. I wish I could have spent more time with her alone, but Mr. and Mrs. Kawahara soon came back into the room, and Mrs. Kawahara served lunch.

It was hard to tell what Mrs. Kawahara was like, since she was in the kitchen most of the time. But Mr. Kawahara loved to talk, even though his English was somewhat surreal. He was a man of medium size with thinning hair, a broad smile, and some nervous mannerisms. He had a way of sucking his breath through his teeth that caught my attention so that I was constantly waiting for it. Later someone told me that it was a typical nervous habit of Japanese.

One evening Mrs. Murata and I met Mr. Kawahara and a friend of his, a Korean novelist, for dinner. During dinner, Kawahara commented that the Japanese were nervous because they were constantly paying attention to interpersonal relationships—always watching for signs, being alert to body language, listening for the slightest nuance. "I'm a very nervous man," he said. "I get very tired from meetings like this."

He compared the Japanese attention to subtlety to the Western communication style. Americans in particular, he said, were much more likely to say directly what was on their minds rather than drop subtle hints. In my opinion, it's a matter of degree. I have read studies indicating that 85 percent of what we Americans really say to each other is communicated by tone of voice and body language; the actual words count for little. With the Japanese, this is taken to the extreme.

"Japanese have 'wet' personalities," Kawahara said. "Americans have 'dry' personalities."

Kawahara believed in blood types as personality indicators, too. Most Japanese had Type A blood, he claimed, while most Americans had Type B—another way of accounting for differences in their personalities. Such a notion was new to me; I couldn't remember my blood type, which he found as amazing as if I had said I didn't know my astrological sign.

Weeks later I received a nice letter from him. "I had a good time with you in this country," he wrote. "I accepted your inner messages, or hints. Your attitudes as to human relations are modest and moderate, so to speak, something like 'Let it be' or 'As it is.' "

Maybe my personality wasn't so "dry" after all.

Yuasa Family

Whatever the problems of a cross-cultural marriage, Mr. and Mrs. Yuasa seem to have adjusted. They met in England years ago, where they were both in graduate school—he from Japan, she from Germany—and fell in love. Then she went to teach in Africa, and he went to New York. For two years they wrote to each other every day, and once he visited her in the Cameroons. They decided that if the relationship could withstand separation, it could prosper if they were together. Over parental objections, they married.

Now they have two daughters, aged twelve and ten. Mr. Yuasa teaches college English; Mrs. Yuasa holds German classes in her living room. They don't own a car, but they have bicycles, and the city bus stops nearby. Several years ago they built their home on a tiny plot of land, an interesting blend of East and West. The girls share a room and sleep on bunk beds; Mr. and Mrs. Yuasa have a Western-style bed in their own room. One small room is crammed with Mr. Yuasa's books. The other is a mat room with a book-lined wall, the titles all in German, where I slept on a futon. There are a sofa and chairs in the living room and a Black Forest cuckoo clock on the wall.

Mrs. Yuasa is a buxom woman with reddish hair and a hearty manner. I didn't have much time to spend with her (her husband brought me home late after a long session with an English conversation club, and Mrs. Kahata picked me up the next morning after breakfast), but we talked fast while she fixed ham and eggs and toasted some good rye bread. She described her Japanese as "homemade, sort of hand-knit." Her daughters spoke Japanese and some English, but she had not made any attempt to teach them German, because, she said, "I don't want to confuse them." I asked if the girls had any problems socially, since the Japanese were often tough on people who were different in any way. But she claimed they had been well accepted by the Japanese, who didn't even call them *gaijin*. The younger girl, an outgoing child, was selected by the pupils in her class to give a talk, a sign of acceptance.

Mrs. Yuasa is an outspoken critic, in a rather blunt way, of Japanese society, but she also seems to have become the spokeswoman for the feelings of many Japanese women. When Japanese housewives gather in her living room to practice German, they talk about what is on their minds. They feel it's safe to open up to her. She says they are afraid of change; there's less risk in doing things the same old way. She often challenges them: "Look, do you really want to change, or do you just want to *talk* about it?"

"The Japanese are the prisoners of group pressure to an extent you wouldn't believe," she said. The weather is uncomfortably hot and humid until well into September, but at about the time of the equinox, everyone switches from summer to fall clothes, no matter what the temperature. Nobody wants to be the one who continues to wear summer clothes when everyone else has changed to fall clothes. One hot fall day a neighbor came to visit dressed in heavy clothes, looked at Mrs. Yuasa's sleeveless blouse, and said, "I envy you the freedom to wear what you want to wear!"

"Now these are people in their own homes," Mrs. Yuasa said, "not in banks or offices where people wear uniforms. Even at home, people still don't dare dress for comfort. And if there happens to be a cold snap before the equinox, people won't put on long sleeves or sweaters." She described a TV news program that showed one of the major intersections in Tokyo on a cold summer day, with crowds of people going in all directions, every one of them shivering in short sleeves—except for one woman who was comfortably dressed for the weather. "When the woman turned around, it was apparent that she was a foreigner—probably an American.

"I try not to abuse my freedom," she said, "but it does give me special privileges in terms of speaking my mind. My students plead with me 'Tell us what it's like! Tell us how we can do it!' " She protests that she would rather not make speeches, that she is not fluent in Japanese, that any one of them can surely say it better—but they all refuse to speak up. It's not their place, they say.

I mentioned my impression that the role of the mother-in-law is no longer as strong in Japan. "Don't believe it," she said. Then she told me the story of a young man and his wife who were planning to build a house together. The wife was very excited until she found that her husband and his mother were making all the decisions—even about the kitchen, where the wife would be doing all the work. She had no say in any of it.

To keep conversation stimulated in her German classes, Mrs. Yuasa clips out news items and posts them on the wall mounted on orange cardboard. One that got a strong reaction was about the decision of a young couple to cancel their expensive wedding ceremony at the last moment. They sent out notices to the invited guests that they were planning a simple wedding and would instead send the hundreds of thousands of yen to a charitable group raising money for the hungry in Africa. The guests were highly critical of the young couple, the news item reported.

Mrs. Yuasa's students were not critical, but they didn't think such behavior would be possible for them personally. "It may have been all right for them," the women agreed, "but we could never do anything like that."

I don't know what Mrs. Yuasa's life as a *gaijin* is really like, to what extent she feels isolated. But she seemed to have tapped into a vein of dissatisfaction that until recently had been deeply buried. She had been accepted as the one who could safely speak out on subjects that lay beneath the surface. She said what the Japanese women dared not say.

Takagi Family

It was in Albuquerque that I first met Mrs. Takagi, a writer of contemporary Japanese fiction touring the United States to gather background material for her next novel. Although her English was not bad, she was traveling with an interpreter, a Japanese woman now living in California who had changed her name from Masako to Martha. It was the end of this part of her trip: Mrs. Takagi was on her way to meet her husband for some skin diving in the Florida Keys, and Martha was flying back to Los Angeles. I invited the two women to join me for breakfast before they left.

189

We sat in a shady patio, talking about the differences in Mrs. Takagi's life as a writer in Japan versus mine in the United States. Martha filled in the blanks when Mrs. Takagi's vocabulary failed. Then the subject shifted to families. I asked if she had children. Mrs. Takagi looked away, and Martha answered for her.

"She had a son. She no longer has him."

I instantly regretted asking the question and mumbled an apology of some sort. "When she divorced her first husband, she had to agree to give up her son, never to see him again," Martha explained. "And she had to pay a large sum of money for his education."

This seemed like a shocking kind of settlement to me, but I was not about to ask any more questions. A month later, I got a letter from Mrs. Takagi, inviting me to visit her in Fukuoka. She would find a hotel room for me if I would spend the evening with her and her husband. I wrote back and accepted.

Before I saw her again, I found out more about divorce in Japan. I had told her story to the women at Mrs. Yoshida's and asked what they thought. "It's possible," one of the women suggested, "that infidelity is the reason she can't see her son. She would be seen, especially by her former in-laws, as an immoral woman. Her mother-in-law might have claimed the child."

"It's a double standard," one of the other wives said. "Men are allowed to play around, particularly the wealthy ones who can support a mistress. That's all right in Japan, but it's not all right for a woman to have a lover. She can lose her child."

It was near the end of my trip when I reached Fukuoka and called Mrs. Takagi. She was planning what she called a "home party" to entertain me and some Americans she knew from the American Center. I hoped she'd invite me to come to her apartment and help her, or at least keep her company in the kitchen that afternoon, but that wasn't the Japanese style. So I walked around in the rain for a while and killed time until her husband came to pick me up for the five-minute walk to their home.

Mr. Takagi is a lawyer, a rare breed in Japan. Japan is not a litigious society—the Japanese don't make much use of lawyers. Someone has said that there are fewer attorneys practicing law in Japan than there are in the state of Illinois. The Japanese don't have elaborate contracts and rarely sue each other, maybe because the population is so homogeneous and the society so rigidly structured that contracts and lawsuits aren't necessary. A Japanese woman who has lived in the U.S. for several years offered an explanation for the legal behavior of Americans: In the United States, with its many ethnic groups who think and do business in certain ways, lawyers are the bridges between different kinds of people and different styles of thinking.

Apparently there was enough business in Fukuoka, the largest city on the island of Kyushu, to afford Mr. Takagi a good living. Their condominium, on the top floor of a new brick building, was lavishly furnished Western-style. The only way I knew I was in a Japanese home was that all the guests were in their stocking feet, their shoes parked out by the door. When Mr. Takagi offered me a drink, I asked for sake. He laughed and humored me, but instead of serving it warm in a tiny ceramic cup, he handed it to me "on the rocks," the American way of drinking. The food was French and so was the wine—extremely expensive in Japan. Mrs. Takagi produced escargots (snails) in garlic butter, beef stew made with wine, French bread, and fancy dessert served in an orange peel cut to look like a basket. Later, for fun, they passed around freeze-dried "astronaut food," which she had picked up at the Space Center in Houston.

191

Mr. and Mrs. Takagi seemed to live a nontraditional life: a second marriage, a Western-style home, lots of travel to the United States, French food, and wine. But not everything was un-Japanese: Mrs. Takagi's mother-in-law lived with them.

Epilogue:
Putting It
All Together

A lot had happened in a month. I had become accustomed to some of the superficial aspects of life in Japan. I was now fairly adept at getting in and out of shoes and slippers. Bowing seemed as natural as shaking hands. I could get around Tokyo easily on the subway, and I had ridden trains all over the country, having been able to find my way around as long as the signs were written in *romaji*. I used my few phrases of *Nihongo* unselfconsciously and promised myself that someday I would learn to speak the language properly. Maybe I would even learn to write some of the beautiful, mysterious *kanji*.

On the day I was to leave, Maiko-chan and Mr. Shirota came by to share one last meal. It was after the equinox, and Maiko had changed to a cool-weather wardrobe, a stylish woolen skirt and jacket; she wore her hair a new way. Mr. Shirota wanted to take me to the plane, and I gratefully accepted his offer. It was a cumbersome trip to the airport, ninety minutes from Tokyo by bus or airport limousine; taxis were prohibitively expensive. His appearance on the last day was as welcome as it had been on the first.

I had accumulated more than I could carry. When I left for Japan, one section of my suitcase was filled with gifts, the handwoven mats I presented to people who had been kind and hospitable. But, as already mentioned, in Japan one gift always deserves another, and my hosts and hostesses had given me presents in return. When I had visited the *kendo* class, the elderly *kendo* master (who spoke a little English) had promised to send me calligraphy that he would execute for me personally. A week later it had been delivered to my hotel, beautifully matted and framed, addressed to "Mrs. C. Mayu," and much too large to fit into either of my bags. Someone else had given me an elegant book of Japanese art, lovely but heavy. By the time I was ready to leave, I could no longer carry my own luggage, which now included two *meishi* cases, some jewelry, innumerable examples of calligraphy (unframed), a wood carving of the three monkeys (See No Evil, Speak No Evil, Hear No Evil), two embroidered balls, a carved mirror, and assorted books and pictures.

I had acquired other things as well. Instead of handwriting all my notes as I had on previous trips, I had talked into a miniature tape recorder at the end of each day. The result was hours and hours of tapes that I had to get home safely and then transcribe. Before I left Utsunomiya, Mrs. Murata had taken me on the rounds of the board of education offices so that I could bow and thank people who had been connected with my visits to schools. She mailed the list to my hotel in Tokyo, along with the names and addresses of people who had helped me out in other ways—and they were legion. When I got home I wrote thank-you notes to everyone. I have since heard from most of these people, letters or Christmas cards or New Year's greetings, many of them enclosing copies of snapshots they had taken while I was there.

I never heard from Gina, and since her address was not one of those included by Mrs. Murata, I haven't written to her. I think of her often, though—a fine example of someone whose experience living in another culture had helped her to understand her own culture—and herself—better. As I've worked on this book, putting the pieces together, I've often thought of what someone had said to her about Japan:

"When you've been in Japan for seven days, it all seems very strange, and you realize you don't understand how the society works at all. Then when you've been in Japan for seven months, you think you've got it all figured out. And when you've been in Japan for seven years, you realize that you don't understand it at all."

But what a challenge to try!

February 1, 1988
Albuquerque, New Mexico

Glossary

Pronunciation guide to Japanese vocabulary

Ainu (EYE-nooh)—aboriginal peoples of Japan

bento (BEHN-toh)—box lunch

buraku-min (B'RAHK-meen)—literally "village people"; also called *eta*

chan (CHAHN)—affectionate form of address for children

daimyo (DY-myoh)—feudal baron

eta (EH-tah)—those traditionally of the lowest caste; also called *buraku-min*

futon (wh'TOHN)—floor mattress

gaijin (GY-jeen)—outsider; foreigner

geisha (GAY-shah)—woman trained to amuse men

haiku (HY-kooh)—17-syllable poem about nature

hajime masaite (HAH-jee-meh MAHSH-teh)—greetings, like "How do you do?"

hashi (HAH-shee)—chopsticks

hogoshi (HOH-goh-shee)—volunteer parole worker

ijime (EE-jee-meh)—student bullying

ikebana (EE-keh-bah-nah)—art of flower arranging

itadaki masu (EE-tah-dah-kee mahss)—"let us be grateful"; said before meals

juku (JOOH-kooh)—private tutoring school

Kabuki (KAH-booh-kee)—traditional Japanese theater

kami (KAH-mee)—gods worshiped in ancient Japan

Kamikaze (KAH-mee-kah-zeh)—"divine wind"; suicide pilots in World War II

kampyo (KAHM-pyoh)—dried gourd used in making *sushi*

kana (KAH-nah)—phonetic system for writing Japanese

kanji (KAHN-jee)—Chinese characters used to write Japanese

karaoke (KAH-rah-oh-keh)—bar in which customers pay to sing

ken (KEHN)—prefecture, similar to a state

kendo (KEHN-doh)—fencing with wooden swords

kimono (KEE-moh-noh)—traditional Japanese robe

kyoiku mama (KYOH-ee-kooh mama)—"education mama"

Kyozo (KYOH-zoh)—storage place for Buddhist scriptures

meishi (MAY-shee)—business card

miso (MEE-soh)—fermented bean paste used to make broth

mochi (MOH-chee)—pounded rice

natto (NAH-toh)—fermented soybeans

Nihon (NEE-hohn)—literally, "land of the rising sun"; Japan

Nihongo (NEE-hohn-goh)—Japanese language

Nippon (NEE-pohn)—another name for Japan

nori (NOH-ree)—seaweed

obi (OH-bee)—sash worn with *kimono*

okonomi-yaki (OH-koh-noh-mee–yah-kee)—chopped meat and vegetables in a kind of pancake *origami* (OH-ree-gah-mee)—art of paper folding

pachinko (PAH-cheen-koh)—game of chance resembling vertical pinball machine

romaji (ROH-mah-jee)—Roman alphabet, used to write Japanese

ronin (ROH-neen)—masterless *samurai*; students who have failed entrance exams and are preparing to take them again

sake (SAH-keh)—rice wine

samurai (SAH-mooh-ry)—warriors or knights who served *daimyo*

san (SAHN)—form of address; Mr., Mrs., or Miss

sarariman (SAH-rah-ree-mahn)—"salaryman"; white-collar employee

sashimi (SAH-shee-mee)—thinly sliced raw fish

sensei (SEHN-say)—teacher

shochu (SHOH-chooh)—clear liquor resembling vodka

shōgun (SHOH-gun)—military dictator; chief of *daimyo*

shoji (SHOH-jee)—translucent paper partition

soroban (SOH-roh-bahn)—abacus, a device for doing arithmetical calculations

sumo (S'MOH)—wrestlers known for their enormous weight

sushi (SOOH-shee)—specially prepared rice, often served with raw fish

taibatsu (TY-bahts)—corporal punishment in schools

tanshin funin (TAHN-sheen wh'neen)—man who lives apart from his family

tatami (TAH-tah-mee)—compressed straw mats

tempura (TEHM-pooh-rah)—fish or vegetables dipped in batter and deep-fried

tofu (TOH-wh'ooh)—soybean curd

tokonoma (TOH-koh-noh-mah)—alcove in traditional Japanese room

torii (TOH-ree)—gateway to Shinto shrine
yakitori (YAH-kee-toh-ree)—chicken grilled on skewers
yobiko (YOH-bee-koh)—cram school for entrance exams
yukata (YOOH-kah-tah)—cotton robe like *kimono*

Pronunciation guide to Japanese place names

Edo (EH-doh)—"eastern capital"; early name for Tokyo
Fukuoka (WHOO-kwoh-kah)—largest city on Kyushu
Ginza (GEEN-zah)—famous shopping area of Tokyo
Harajuku (HAH-rah-jooh-kooh)—fashionable area of
   Tokyo
Hiroshima (HEE-roh-shee-mah)—city in western Honshu;
   destroyed by atomic bomb in 1945
Hokkaido (HOH-ky-doh)—northernmost of four main
   islands
Honshu (HOHN-shooh)—largest of four main islands
Ibaraki-ken (EE-bah-rah-kee kehn)—one of Japan's
   forty-seven prefectures
Kamakura (KAH-mah-kooh-rah)—area of shrines and
   temples near Tokyo
Kyoto (KYOH-toh)—early imperial capital; on Honshu
Kyushu (KYOOH-shooh)—the farthest south and west of
   the four main islands
Mito (MEE-toh)—city in Ibaraki-ken
Miyazaki (MEE-yah-zah-kee)—city in southern Kyushu
Nagasaki (NAH-gah-sah-kee)—city in Kyushu
Nara (NAH-rah)—ancient capital, predating Kyoto
Niigata (NEE-gah-tah)—main port on west coast of
   northern Honshu
Nikko (NEE-koh)—resort area of temples and shrines in
   Tochigi-ken

Okinawa (OH-kee-nah-wah)—one of many small islands
   belonging to Japan
Osaka (OH-sah-kah)—important commercial and industrial
   city
Roppongi (ROH-pohn-gee)—neighborhood in Tokyo
Shikoku (SH'-koh-kooh)—smallest of four main islands
Tochigi-ken (TOH-chee-gee kehn)—one of Japan's
   forty-seven prefectures
Tokyo (TOH-kyoh)—Japan's capital and largest city
Tsukuba Science City (TS-KOOH-bah)—scientific
   community established by government in eastern
   Honshu
Utsunomiya (OOHT-s'noh-mee-yah)—prefectural capital of
   Tochigi-ken
Yokohama (YOH-koh-hah-mah)—second-largest city in
   Japan
Yoyogi Park (YOH-yoh-gee)—popular park in Tokyo

Further Reading

Hidden Differences: Doing Business with the Japanese. Edward T. Hall and Mildred Reed Hall (Garden City: Anchor Press/Doubleday, 1987)

Japanese Education Today. U.S. Department of Education (Washington, D.C.: U.S. Government Printing Office, 1987)

Japan's High Schools. Thomas P. Rohlen (Berkeley: University of California Press, 1983)

On Becoming Japanese: The World of the Preschool Child. Joy Hendry (University of Hawaii Press)

The Chrysanthemum and the Sword: Patterns of Japanese Culture. Ruth Benedict (New York: New American Library, 1946)

The Japanese. Edwin O. Reischauer (Cambridge: Harvard University Press, 1977)

The Japanese Mind. Robert C. Christopher (New York: Fawcett Columbine, 1983)

Index